LET THE REASON BE
LOVE

LET THE REASON BE LOVE

A Song of Faith

MERRILL OSMOND

and

Janice Barrett Graham

Published by:
Tidal Wave Books
Pleasant Grove, UT 84062
www.tidalwavebooks.com

Journal entries have been edited for clarity.

Book design by Camille G. Turpin
Back inside flap photo courtesy of Jane Malcom

Second Printing, August 2003
Third Printing, January 2004
Printed in Korea by USAsia Press

Library of Congress Cataloging-in-Publication Data

Osmond, Merrill. Graham, Janice Barrett.
Let the Reason Be Love: A Song of Faith.
Merrill Osmond and Janice Barrett Graham.
1st edition.

ISBN, print edition: 0-9724770-0-4

1. Memoir—Merrill Osmond
2. Inspiration—Religious
3. Entertainment—Music

Library of Congress Control Number: 2002112842

Dedicated to

my parents George Virl Osmond Sr. and Olive Davis Osmond
who have shown unwavering faith in me over the years

my brothers Virl, Tom, Alan, Wayne, Jay, Donny, and Jimmy
who have stood by me through tough times

my sister Marie
whose courage in overcoming obstacles I greatly admire

my son Travis
who is a shining example to his brothers and sisters

my son Justin
who shows unconditional love for all people

my son Shane
whose talent and intelligence amaze me

my daughter Heather
in whose presence I am humbled

my son Troy
who stands as a beacon of light

my daughter Sheila
who is my teacher

and to my dear wife Mary
who has endured much living with a man like me

Preface

I started and stopped work on this book many times for various reasons over the last ten years. My assistants and close friends became frustrated with me for changing directions time and time again. But despite every kind of delay, my underlying faith in a particular finished project never wavered. Then recently, new avenues opened. Everything seemed to fall into place, moving the project forward at a rapid pace. Out of a jumble of material, a readable book took shape over the relatively short period of a few months. Looking back, I find I wouldn't have wanted things to happen any other way.

The erratic progress of the book itself is a metaphor for what I hope to share in its contents — that the leaps and tumbles, the highs and lows, the dead ends and open roads I have experienced in my life, and continue to experience, are all part of a loving Heavenly Father's plan for my progress. Through all my struggles, I have had the opportunity to enjoy the most desirable of all feelings, God's love, and to learn to press on each day because of that love.

Some may be surprised at the experiences I reveal in this book. Nevertheless, I have felt compelled to relate them in the hope of sharing what has given me such comfort and motivation. My challenges continually bring me joy and strength as my eyes are opened to their greater purpose and meaning. This is my prayer for my readers as well.

I testify that divine love is available to anyone who honestly seeks it, and that the truths we can glean from that source are applicable to everyday life. I have felt that assurance through every step of preparing this book.

Contents

Timeline

1953   Born in Ogden, Utah

1957   Osmond Brothers Quartet formed

1962–1968   Appeared on *The Andy Williams Show*

1971–1976   Enjoyed height of pop music fame

1973   Married, September 17

1975–1986   Children Arrived

1976–1979   Produced *The Donny and Marie Show*

1981–1990   Recorded, wrote, and produced

1982–1984   Performed on U.S. tours with brothers

1992–2002   Performed in Branson, Missouri, and on tours and cruise lines with brothers

1993   Relocated family to Branson

1997   Moved family back to Utah

2003   Performing at Andy Williams Moon River Theater in Branson, and on tours and cruise lines with Wayne and Jay

Merrill Osmond, age 20

Tidal Wave Books

LET THE REASON BE
LOVE

Show Time

Journal, age 20

It's Madison Square Garden, New York City, the one place my brothers and I have been looking forward to for years. We have three diesel trucks full of equipment waiting to be unloaded. I have a terrible cold, just what I need. A doctor came and gave me a shot. Then I walked around the whole place — it took me about 45 minutes. It's so big it's scary. Our concert is sold out and everyone is on edge. Camera crews are gathering outside. There are break-ins everywhere — girls are trying to get to us. What would they do if they caught us? Strange thought. We heard something about a bomb threat. The police arrived and had dogs check out the entire building. Dinner was served for the brothers, but I was so sick I couldn't eat a thing.

Later. I'm taking the time to write one more time before the show. Half hour to go. Our sound man is still trying to get the system working. Our manager is ticked and someone might get fired. I've never seen so much purple. Purple hats, dresses, socks and banners. There is screaming everywhere: "We want the Osmonds! We want the Osmonds!" And it's very weird. It's what you have always wanted, and then when it's here, you want to run and hide from it. Everyone is pacing. Our father is nervous. The brothers just called everyone into our room for a tech meeting.

Five minutes. Everything is now ready to go. The sound company finally got up and running. Our manager told everyone to leave the room so we could get our thoughts together. We locked the door and offered a prayer to Heavenly Father that we might have a good and safe show.

Later. No words can really describe what happened tonight. When my brothers and I hit the stage the noise blew us away. The decibel level was so loud our ears started to ache – and we were wearing ear plugs! Does that say everything? But the thing that completely overwhelmed me was 20,000 screaming people all taking flash pictures at the same time. I felt like I was moving in slow motion under a huge strobe light for two solid hours.

Halfway through the show, I noticed a young guy wearing a ripped t-shirt staring at me. Then I saw he had a gun tucked in his pants. All of our Security were on each side of the stage making sure no one would try

4

to sneak on. This left the front of the stage totally exposed. The thought came to me to stare this kid down like Chuck Norris taught us to do in our karate training. We happened to be doing "One Bad Apple." I was singing the words, "I can tell you've been hurt by that look on your face. Some guy brought a sad end to your happy world. You need love but you're afraid that if you give in, someone else will come along and sock it to you again." Well, this kid got so nervous by the end of the song, he bolted. The police finally saw what was going on and grabbed him.

It's good to be in my hotel room. I am still feeling sick, but I'm happy the show is over. The pressure was almost too much. I'm too young for this stuff – ha.

The year was 1973, decades ago, and it has occurred to me since that I certainly was too young for that kind of pressure. My unusual life in the entertainment business has stretched me beyond my capacity all along the way. But whatever our circumstances, it could be that every one of us feels unprepared when something happens that appears bigger than we can handle, more than we can take in, or outside our experience. These are moments when, like it or not, it's show time. No more dress rehearsals. The spotlight singles us out. Can we pull it off? Will everything go as planned? Can we withstand the stress? And just when we wrap up one huge gig, there will be another, and it will be show time again.

Throughout my years as a performer, I've met all kinds of people who have shared with me all kinds of sad stories. The interesting thing is that everyone's story is basically the same. Our need as human beings for acceptance and meaning screams out from between the lines like a thousand hysterical fans.

My friends, in this book you won't find a chronological account of the Osmonds' rise to fame in the entertainment business, a glowing narrative of my family life, or a comprehensive discourse on the doctrines of my religion. My purpose is to share the simple good news of my faith. With it comes a way to relieve any level of that Madison Square Garden-type pressure and uncertainty we all face in this life, whether it quietly builds up inside us over a period of time or suddenly hits us in the face, too loud, too bright, too real.

Through my own experiences, which may be more similar to yours than you think, I invite you backstage into God's own tech meeting. In it, He instructs us to change the way we see this grand show and our individual performances. He advises us to let go of some of the old routines and try new songs and new steps. He teaches us how to move the spotlight away from ourselves and our experiences, and shine it on His perfect love.

Setting the Stage

PURPOSE

Journal, age 14

On April 30, 1953, in Ogden Utah, I was born into a neat family. George Virl Osmond, Sr., my father, is a very strong and firm individual, but as humble and down-to-earth as any man I've ever met.

Many people over the years have expressed admiration for my family, our togetherness, talent, and toothy smiles. I would be most pleased to be remembered for our faith. Taught by exemplary parents and carefully schooled in our religion, we truly believe in a God who is watching over us and wants only our happiness.

None of this means the Osmond family has always sung perfectly in tune, so to speak. We've had our troubles like any other family. Inevitably, the media-hyped notion of an ideal family caused us to feel unusual pressure. It also caused others to compare their failures to our public successes, their broken or dysfunctional families to the image of our intact home.

Comparing ourselves to others is nothing but a dead end. Unless we live in the other person's, or family's, mind and heart and skin, we simply don't have enough information to make an accurate comparison. It's nothing but a distraction from our own personal development. We are better off facing our own customized circumstances with faith that they exist for our ultimate benefit.

Though some may be a little disappointed, I would like to somewhat dispel the perfect family myth, if there is one, in an effort to shed light on certain truths. Painful as it may be, facing unpleasant realities is necessary to personal progression. But hang with me. It's going to be worthwhile.

It seems everyone deserves a happy childhood as a sort of rehearsal for adult life. Ideally, our younger years serve as an extended, insulated time to learn the tunes and taps that prepare us to perform well when the curtain rises and we are center stage. But a perfect childhood? Chances are, there is no such thing. Even in the best of circumstances, no family is perfect. No parents are perfect. And harsh as it may sound, this is part of God's plan—to send us here to this earth to experience some measure of trouble, beginning with our first breath, our first step, our first day of school.

My upbringing was greatly complicated by the structure, allegiance, and perfectionism required by the lofty goals my parents set for us as a family. It was obvious to me from an early age that what I was experiencing was far different from what children outside my family were experiencing. But it was my family, where I belonged; I accepted my circumstances without question, as children do.

The first home I can recollect was the one-story brick house on North Washington Boulevard in Ogden, Utah where I lived until I was eight. Surrounded by shade trees and built facing the street, it concealed an idyllic one-acre farm where we kept a menagerie of chickens, cows, horses, goats, cats, and dogs; cultivated apple, cherry, plum, and pear trees; and grew a productive vegetable garden.

The Osmond children arrived in a steady stream with plenty of hugs and kisses to go around. One of my fondest memories is jumping onto our parents' bed on a Sunday morning. There were so many of us kids, we tussled for a prime position close to Mother and Father. It didn't matter that I always seemed to end up at the foot of the bed. What mattered was that I felt an essential closeness and security.

Though I had plenty of friends in those early childhood days, I was only allowed to see them at school or church. We never brought our friends home or played in the neighborhood. Father said, "You spend the day with your friends at school, and I think you should devote the rest of your time to your family." We obeyed his wishes rather than risk his disapproval. I remember the canal that ran along the far end of our property where I sometimes saw the neighbor kids splashing and squealing. I don't recall ever being near that canal except once when I watched the police pull out a drowned man who had tried to escape from the reform school across the fence.

On the bright side, even though I missed out on a normal social life, my brothers and I learned to work together, play together, and confide in each other. We were best friends, developing relationships which became invaluable in our shared show business career.

We boys were kept pretty well in line with an orderly regimen, almost like boot camp. We were each assigned our own footlocker, closet, and single bed in a big dormitory-like room. Father espoused a work ethic that proved unstoppable. Lights went out every night at eight o'clock; we awoke, often at 4:00 A.M., to Alan playing reveille on the trumpet. This structure was necessary in order to get our farm chores done in time to shower, eat breakfast, and head off to school.

To get the chores done Father set us up in what he called "strings." The first string consisted of Virl, Tom, Alan, and Wayne. Smack in the middle, I was in charge of the second string as they came along: Jay, Donny, Marie, and Jimmy. I always watched disappointed when Father and the older guys piled in our old green flat-bed truck and drove noisily off to haul hay or sugar beets while we younger ones were left to weed the radishes and string beans.

But having four older brothers had its advantages. I watched them do most of the hard work and from my viewpoint they made it look easy and worthwhile. Seeing my brothers toiling side by side on the farm perhaps set the stage for a lifetime of working together to accomplish common goals.

My father made a living by operating a real estate business and the local post office. In addition to our chores at home, we children were enlisted to lend a hand in stamping, sorting, and bagging packages, especially during the Christmas holidays. After school we'd go directly to the post office and work until dark. But I had a secret even darker than the winter night outside. I never quite caught on exactly how to sort the mail into different city postal codes. Sorry to say, I mostly guessed.

Fear of my father's disapproval kept me from asking for help at the post office. Lackadaisical attitudes or mediocrity of any kind were unacceptable in the Osmond family. I figured if Father found out I didn't know what I was doing, I would be out of there fast. But I wanted to please him, to be a big guy, and do a man's work. Even though the mail probably found its way to its destination, my little-boy heart beat with fear and shame.

Much later, I found out that fear is a poor motivator. In this instance it kept me from enjoying myself, making progress, and truly doing my best. It's a safe bet our relationships are always more important than the job or particular problem at hand. It could be that if the accomplishment of a chore or fulfillment of a duty damages a relationship, the greatest blessings for doing it have been lost. I know God Himself would much rather I perform out of love than fear.

Starting in kindergarten, I became the target of a fourth grade bully who was so intimidating I made up every story in the book to get out of going to school. He was big and buff with a butch haircut and a scar running from one eye to the corner of his mouth. His verbal threats and body language toward me were so frightening, I was sure this kid was going to kill me and bury me in a ditch somewhere. I also knew how my father felt about such things. If I complained he would only get after me saying, "C'mon, grow up, get tough." The persecution continued unchecked for years.

One night my father must have heard me crying in my bed. Through my tears I saw him standing there asking me what was wrong. After hearing my sad tale he enfolded me in his arms and held me tight.

"Why didn't you come to me before?" he asked.

At a loss, I answered, "Because you're so busy."

"No, not for this kind of thing," he said. My father then proceeded to do all in his power to remedy the situation. He talked to the principal of my school who had the boy publicly apologize. Though he kept his eye on me, the bully never bothered me again. We moved shortly after that.

I dearly love and respect my father. He is an outstanding man embodying many characteristics truly representative of our Father in Heaven. It's a sure thing, though, that all earthly fathers make mistakes; I was to learn this when I became a father myself. How comforting to know our Heavenly Father is perfect and does not make mistakes. We can count on His perfect, constant love regardless of our failings.

It wasn't until after I got married that I became aware

of any shortcomings in my upbringing. While it's best we all come to the rude awakening that life isn't picture perfect, this reality check must not discount the good things in our lives. I am everlastingly grateful for the learning opportunities I continue to glean from my family's strengths, as well as its weaknesses.

What a blessing to have parents who instilled in me the glorious truth that I am a child of God. They raised me not only to see myself as a child of God, but to see everyone else as God sees them. This perspective gave me the beginnings of a humble, child-like faith I could apply to every experience I was to encounter in my life.

The truth is, this world is not our original home, our parents not our original parents. We are children of loving eternal parents, a Father and Mother in Heaven. We lived with Them in a pre-earth life. Our Father wants what every good, successful father wants for his children: to grow to be happy and successful like Him. So He devised a plan to send us to earth and learn by our own invaluable experience.

Concerning this plan, one prominent son, Satan, said he would force us to do everything correctly, and in so doing take all the glory for himself. But Jesus supported Heavenly Father's plan. Knowing we would learn best by making our own choices, many of which would be faulty, he offered to sacrifice himself to pay for our sins. This gift opens the way for us to qualify through repentence to be in the presence of our Heavenly Father again. In addition, he would do it all to give glory to his Father, showing the way of true happiness for us to follow. To assure we would truly be tested, we all agreed that a veil of forgetfulness would separate us here on earth from our heavenly pre-existence.

With this eternal perspective, childhood's inconsistencies take on new meaning. If we had a perfect memory of our true value to God our Father and His Son, Jesus Christ, we would treat one another with nothing but patience and respect. But we are put here on earth as mortal beings, children and parents alike. Childhood, with its injustices, is part of the plan for us to learn and grow. It's like the father who lets go of his small son's wobbling bicycle knowing he may fall, but also giving him the chance to learn to ride it. Our Father allows us to make our own decisions in an all-wise act of divine charity.

Just as I described my father in my early journal entry as a strong, firm, humble person, we can be sure every righteous quality resides in the person of our Father in Heaven. The essence of His wish for us, and the purpose of our earthly existence, is to give us the opportunity to work toward becoming as marvelous as He is.

In the Wings

SUSTENANCE

Journal, age 14

My mother is as sweet and as perfect in my eyes as any angel in heaven.

The fact that we have a Father in Heaven makes the idea of a Mother in Heaven not only logical, but obvious. Perhaps She is so cherished by our Heavenly Father that He gives us no name by which to call Her, in this way keeping Her protected from any disrespect. My earthly mother was a lovely prototype of our divinely reverenced Mother.

While my father was the taskmaster, my mother was the visionary. A deeply spiritual person, she encouraged me to search out and learn of God's plan for me. Mother believed we could use our talents to glorify our Heavenly Father and to share the good news of the gospel of Jesus Christ. Because of this belief, she helped us succeed in any way she could, at the same time giving us children a secure foundation of love and constancy.

Due to the traveling we did as entertainers, we missed a lot of school. Our teachers would prepare the classwork for a week only to find us gone for two weeks. This would foul up our assignments and leave us behind. To catch us up, Mother had Father rig a schoolroom for us in the attic of our house, complete with desks, chairs, and a chalkboard. She gave us lessons and hired other people to assist when her skills were lacking.

In our house, every Friday was "family night." We planned gatherings such as Mother's famous candlelight dinners where we ate like kings, downing twenty ears of homegrown corn on the cob at one sitting. Often we put on shows, singing and dancing together, performing for each other and our grandparents.

A favorite outing was hopping in the station wagon and heading off to the drive-in movie. We'd get our pajamas on, fix popcorn and drinks, and sometimes cut up a watermelon to take with us. Lying on our sleeping bags, we gazed at the stars and fell sound asleep long before the movie ended.

But togetherness can go too far. Take our clothes for instance. It wasn't enough that we four brothers had to dress in identical costumes for performances. Mother also sewed identical church and school clothes for all of us, tagging every item we wore with color-coded labels. To her, sewing in bulk was economical, and the color code was one sure way to know immediately who had left their clothes on the bathroom floor — a big deal when a large family shares one bathroom. Virl had blue, Tom red, Alan yellow, Wayne orange, me purple, and Jay green.

I got used to the color coding, and purple sort of became my identity. That's the way it was until one day thirteen-year-old Donny, who had never had a color like us older boys, casually mentioned in *Tiger Beat,* a teen star magazine, that he liked purple. His fans caught on with a passion and that was the end of purple for me. There went my shorts. I was sorry to lose my favorite purple silk shirt Mom made for me too.

From then on, Donny, a.k.a. Captain Purple, became inseparably associated with my color. I chose black after that and to this day, I have a closet full of black clothes. Could be I'm still mourning my lost color. It was just a little thing, but it wasn't the only time I would be called upon to defer to my brother Donny.

Whenever anything happened that seemed to devalue me as a person, my mother would always smile and encourage me to keep going, to use the experience to become a better person. In her own life, she had a way of sizing up the test, turning to the Lord for guidance, and dealing with it as best she could. "This too shall pass," she'd always say. This phrase helped me through all kinds of difficult problems when I felt discouraged.

God loves us so much that in the middle of our challenges he gives us things like cuddling in our parents' bed, corn on the cob, drive-in movies, and mothers like mine. That's the way this amazing world is set up. If everybody and everything were perfect, we wouldn't have the chance to learn. But our Father in Heaven is merciful and gives us plenty to enjoy in between the hard lessons. According to the plan, our enjoyment is increased because of our difficulties. My mother knows this.

Mother's faith is her greatest gift. Perhaps that veil of forgetfulness is especially thin around her, for she knows of a better world; she has seen it in her dreams. Not only did she teach her children, but in the middle of our glitzy show business lifestyle, she took every opportunity to befriend others and testify of her beliefs.

I remember a time as a young child trying to get my mother's attention for some little thing. She was busy talking to an Osmond fan on the telephone about Heavenly Father and His love for us. I sat there for a good half hour waiting. It was nothing new. This was my mother who never tired of sharing the comforting and strengthening truths of the gospel with anyone, including strangers.

At a royal command performance in 1974, I watched my mother hand the Queen of England a copy of sacred scripture, The Book of Mormon: Another Testament of Jesus Christ, which we use alongside the Holy Bible. I knew right then and there that she was not afraid of what the world would think of her, only what her Father in Heaven thought. She also gave Elvis Presley, whom she visited with many times, information regarding our faith and our church, The Church of Jesus Christ of Latter-day Saints (LDS). Elvis read The Book of Mormon; he wrote in it, making notations and comments throughout its pages. It was given to our family and later donated to the LDS Church Historical Department.

Journal, age 48, Branson, Missouri

I just hung up from talking to Father and Mother. I felt the need to call them for some reason. It was about 11:00 P.M. and I woke them up as usual. There were two very cheerful voices on the other end of the line. Mother seemed to be especially interested in each of her children tonight. She also talked specifically of my son, Justin, and the needs of the hearing impaired, research for the deaf and how to get the word out. She was at the peak of her creativity. She talked about her kids finally coming home to live a more peaceful life, to find joy in the simple things. We talked about each member of the family starting with Virl and ending with Jimmy. She seemed so concerned for the welfare of each of us.

The next morning. I was awakened at 8:00 A.M. by a pounding on the door. The phone started ringing as well. Both Jay and Wayne wanted to tell me that Mother is in the hospital having had some kind of stroke. All members of the family have been contacted to start making arrangements to go home. It turns out that Mother fell down in her condo and was taken by ambulance to the St. George Hospital. This is very serious.

Later that day. Donny just called. Mother was

hemorrhaging in her head and life-flighted by helicopter to Provo for surgery. Father is very fragile. The brothers sent Jimmy home and three of us will take over here in Branson until further notice.

By the end of that day I was on a plane headed back to Utah, praying the entire way. When I arrived at the hospital most of the family was there.

Mother's recovery is proving to be slow but sure. We children often take turns sitting with her. During one night, months after her stroke, when I was all alone with Mother singing her some hymns, she rolled over to one side, opened her pretty eyes and looked at me as if to say something, but the tubes down her throat prevented her from speaking. Instead, she reached up with her left arm and tapped the pillow on her right side. I didn't understand. I hurried and found paper and pencil. On it she wrote, "Lie down and I'll rub your hair." A tear slipped down both our faces. Looking into her eyes, I expressed my deep feelings for her. She squeezed my hand in answer, three times. I love you.

Journal, age 13

Our first airplane ride. We are going to Sweden. It was sad having to say goodbye to Mother. The stewardesses were laughing at us because we held on with all we had.

20

Old Routines

AGENCY

Journal, age 13

We have a few hit records here in Sweden, and the people are great. They gave us gifts from their country. I can't seem to memorize any Swedish — everyone else can. Very frustrating. We are working at the Burns Café in Stockholm. I've never worked so hard in my life. We did our show and then walked four flights upstairs to get to our dressing room. Just as we were getting undressed, the audience started to clap again. We looked at each other, got dressed and started back down the stairs. We did another number to make them happy, then walked up the stairs once more. We had to do this four times. My legs are hurting tonight.

When my father discovered that we four little boys could sing harmony, that we could pick out and carry our individual parts, he put his heart into developing our talent. I was only four years old when the family decision was made to seriously pursue a career in show business.

The question arises, should a four-year-old be called upon to make such a decision, a decision which would dramatically affect his life from that day on? No. Unlike others who rise to stardom in the pop music business because of a personal dream or ambition, my career was imposed upon me at an early age. In the old days, my mother used to say I would make a good doctor. I might have.

Once we began seriously focusing on performing, our already well-structured family life became one of strict discipline. Even the most routine activities were militaristically regimented. Whenever we gathered as a family, Father shouted, "Count off!" We lined up and called out our numbers, oldest to youngest, at lightning speed.

The musical emphasis in our home went well beyond our vocal lessons. While Father instructed us in singing harmony, Mother taught us all to play her instrument, the saxophone. We took additional lessons outside the home, each learning to play a different instrument: trumpet, trombone, clarinet, and piano. After lessons, we came home and taught each other what we had learned. Even our older brothers Virl and Tom, who were both severely hearing-impaired, got into the act by taking their own style of lessons. They taught us all to tap dance.

Journal, age 15

We just followed a seal act. The stage was so wet that when we ran on, we starting sliding everywhere! I'll be glad when we can stop wearing tap shoes.

As a child, I performed with my three brothers at restaurants, rodeos, casinos, parties, churches, weddings, boat shows, boxing matches, beauty contests, Lions Clubs, Caterpillar conventions, you name it. Many times I'd come home from school feeling that light-hearted it's-Friday-and-no-homework feeling only to find I had to go straight to bed for a nap. Whether we could sleep or not, a rest was mandatory so we could stay up late for a performance that night.

After supper we'd get into our costumes, pile in the car, and head to Salt Lake City to perform, most often at the Hotel Utah for an audience of thirty people or so. If we were lucky we came home with thirty dollars. But the real treat for us kids was when Father stopped at Dee's Hamburgers on the way back home. I learned early on that show business isn't as exciting as it's cracked up to be. It's a whole lot of work and a whole lot of pressure, and sometimes all you get is a malt. Sometimes you get something much worse.

Journal, age 14

Reno, Nevada. Our opening act was Bertha and Tina, a couple of elephants. When they finished their fifteen minutes, the curtain closed, the lights blacked out, and the band started in on our first number. We were introduced, we ran out, and guess what? There was a huge pile of elephant manure right in front of our microphone stands. We just stood there, our mouths hanging open. All of a sudden two little guys came running out of the wings with a wheel barrow and shovels. After

23

*about five minutes we were able to start. It was a dinner
show, too. Not many big appetites.*

Our break into big time show business came on our
first visit to California. The Lennon Sisters set up a meeting
for us to see Lawrence Welk whom we thought would be
interested in our act. But for some reason, he cancelled.

To help us over our disappointment and perhaps with
motives of his own, Father took us to Disneyland before
we headed home. Of course we were decked out in our
costumes, sticking out like a whole handful of sore thumbs.
Spotting a barbershop quartet as they pedaled through the
park on their bicycle built for four, we gathered with the
crowd when they stopped to perform. As the Dapper Dans
finished a song they noticed us standing there in our bow
ties and suspenders, a miniature barbershop quartet, and
asked if we sang.

It didn't take much arm-twisting to get us to perform
for a ready-made crowd. Father lined us up and sing we
did. After a few numbers the leader of the group said, "Let's
go see our boss, Tommy Walker." We sang him a song, too,
and later performed for Walt Disney himself. Mr. Disney,
delighted by six-year-old Jay's wayward fake mustache,
immediately arranged for us to perform on a show called
"Disneyland after Dark."

Andy Williams' father saw us performing at Disneyland.
We had just returned from California and were back home
in Utah when we got a phone call from Mr. Williams asking

us to please return to the coast right away. I'll never forget that crazy day. Full of anticipation and excitement, we piled in the car and drove straight back.

For the audition, Father dressed us up in boy-sized tuxedos that must have cost him a fortune. After singing a song called "Cecilia," we looked around the room disappointed that no one seemed the least bit impressed. Continuing with our routine, we finally elicited some applause. We watched the producers retreat into a little huddle. Minutes later, Bob Finkle and Andy Williams asked us to appear on at least one show. It wasn't long before we signed a long-term contract.

With the vision of show business stronger than ever in their minds, Father and Mother decided to sell the real estate business and move to California. We continued to work the streets of Disneyland for a season before the Andy Williams' deal commenced, eventually buying a house in the San Fernando Valley in a town called Arleta. We made a home of it for the six years we performed on the show. Nine months out of twelve, we worked on TV. In the summertime, we toured all over the world while Mother stayed home with Virl, Tom, and the little ones.

I performed on *The Andy Williams Show* from age eight to fourteen. Glamorous as it may seem, with it came a great deal of stress and uncertainty, especially for a group of young boys. We rehearsed for a new TV program every week. Often, we were introduced to new skills and expected to master them within a matter of days. The pressure was on. If we had nothing special to present to the producers of the show each week, we simply weren't invited to perform.

This kept us on our toes in more ways than one. It was like a game of double dare, Hollywood against the Osmonds. It seemed to us they purposely thought up the most difficult routines imaginable just to test our talent and stamina. Complex barbershop harmonies, rock and roll hits, big band numbers. Tap dancing, ice skating, comedy sketches. Tumbling, juggling, karate. And all kinds of musical instruments we had never tried before.

After the presentation of a new show and a full day of rehearsing, my brothers and I would leave the studio and spend the rest of the night and into the morning perfecting everything we had learned. Ultimately, our father made sure we followed through.

For an upcoming Christmas show with Olympic figure skating gold-medalist Peggy Fleming, the producers suggested we ice skate. None of us had ever set foot on ice but, of course, our father said, "No problem." With that, we were each handed a pair of ice skates and pointed in the direction of a rink in the valley. The rest was up to us.

We practiced every day before school, after school, before rehearsals, after rehearsals for a solid week. We had no time for timidity or caution in what turned out to be a figure skating crash course. We bumped and tumbled, smashed and stashed. Blisters and bruises popped up in places we never thought possible. How we hated those skates!

The day of the performance came. They set up the ice rink in the studio. Warming up, we showed off everything we had learned: flips, shoot the duck, skating backwards, in circles, and with fireworks in our hands. When the cameras rolled, we performed our routine in one take without a hitch. Elated, we went home, made a bonfire in the back yard and burned every one of those skates to a crisp.

Growing up, we didn't have much time to goof off. Even when we were little, if we weren't doing homework, family activities, or chores, we were rehearsing barbershop or practicing musical instruments. As teenagers, rehearsing with our electric guitars was about the closest we got to messing around.

Journal, age 13

Today is a holiday so we are going to practice on our guitars and bass. We stayed in our rehearsal room for twelve hours straight. Alan and Wayne touched each other by accident and got electrocuted. Alan really started bleeding. Jay wouldn't stop playing the drums. It was about 3:00 A.M. when the cops showed up! Our neighbor reported us! This lady is a witch!

As children, we were worked unbelievably hard, and when we got older, we chose to work ourselves even harder in the name of family and perfection—so hard that we lost a lot of ourselves in the process. We believed we belonged to something bigger than our individual selves:

our family. Phrases like I can't, I won't, or I quit were not in our vocabulary. It was all for one and one for all. There were no rebels within the Osmond family. It just wasn't allowed.

Of course it wasn't natural to conform, to continually put personal desires and interests aside in favor of the group. It was our father who kept us in line. He was often stern, critical, and exacting. I suppose he had to be for us to realize our goals.

Journal, age 21

Father had a good talk with us today. He said we're lazy and we like to waste time. Well, we were all mad at the time, but now I see a lot of wisdom in what he was saying. He's a very successful man. So all the brothers went to the orange room and worked on our dance routines for about three or four hours before breaking. Then I started working with Donny and Marie on their new album.

Here we were, individuals with different personalities and needs, yet we were obligated to each other because of our family goals. The mentality was united we stand, divided we fall, and we each carried the unwieldy burden of individual responsibility for mutual success whether we realized it or not.

It wasn't until I was older that the trade-offs that came with my family commitment to show business became apparent. As it may be to some degree in many families, the exploitation I experienced was not without personal consequences later in life.

> *He was told what to do from the age of two:*
> *Don't question the dream. Who am I?*
> *The tear that would lead to a life fearing greed*
> *Has fallen and doesn't know why.*
> *"Don't think. It's okay. Together we're strong."*
> *There's no way to knock down the walls.*
> *The mission is set, the dealer has bet.*
> *It's time now to wind up the dolls.*
> — Merrill Osmond, "Wind up the Dolls," 1985

Remember the two plans presented in our pre-earth life? Satan wanted to force us to do good and Jesus wanted us to have the chance to choose to do good. As we exercise this God-given gift of agency, our Heavenly Father wants us to feel His great love for us, to feel empowered by it, to take charge of our lives by relying on His guiding Spirit.

Ideally, children are given more and more opportunities to think for themselves until they are ready to go out into the world and make all their own choices. Growing up, I didn't get many chances to learn by making my own decisions. Because I didn't have these developmental experiences, I was unprepared for much of my adult decision-making and, consequently, made some unwise judgments. I'm still learning to toss aside those old routines. I'm using my agency to try some entirely new steps.

It's exciting to take charge, to choose my responses, to ask God daily for direction on how to spend my time and energy to best serve Him and others. There is no one to blame but myself for any negative feelings, no one to depend on but the Lord for my happiness. I like how it feels.

Rotten Tomatoes

REJECTION

Journal, age 20

The French version of Hell's Angels broke into our concert tonight. I guess they didn't want to buy tickets, plus their girlfriends were all inside. They smashed the windows and in they came! Potatoes and tomatoes started flying toward us. I got hit and it hurt. It was really something dancing to tight choreography while dodging flying food! One of our Security guys named Patsy wasn't going to put up with it and came up on stage with us. He saw one guy ready to throw a potato and leaped like Superman fist first into the crowd and knocked him out cold. More of them tried to get in through the back by way of the loading dock. Our Security said, "One, two, three!" and opened the door. Two or three heads popped in and then slam went the door! Oh, the headaches they must have had! On their way out of the hall, one of these guys threw a raw egg at Father and hit him in the head. It ruined his hairpiece — he says he has to buy a new one.

31

Although unusual at a concert, episodes like these were really nothing new to the Osmond boys. During our time in school, most of us brothers got beat up at one time or another. I began to wonder if it were for no other reason than that they hated our big smiles.

Before I get into Junior Hell's Angels stories, let me say that school wasn't all bad. I only went to public school from kindergarten to fourth grade, in Utah and in California. After that, we had private tutors. One of the nice things about school was being with friends, especially since our father didn't allow playing after school. In first grade we decorated our bicycles with crepe paper and rode them down Main Street in the town parade. I was also one of those lucky boys who fall in love for the first time with his teacher. It was Mrs. DeFreeze in second grade who first won my heart with her soft voice and flowing auburn hair.

In my few years of public school, most of my friends were girls. Guys mostly made fun of me. I was different simply because they'd seen me on TV. Though I did well in sports and the boys wanted me on their teams, there was a lot of extra pressure on me to play well. If I didn't make points every time, I was thrown out. Even so, I was pretty good at football and chosen for quarterback. We named our team the Golden Eagles, running and tumbling on the school's asphalt playground. Man, it smarted when you got tackled on that blacktop. A big kid knocked me down so hard once that today my knees still feel it. It was totally worth it.

Speaking of getting knocked down, let's go back to bullies. Like I mentioned earlier, I'd had experience with persecution starting in kindergarten when the threatening fourth grader singled me out. Because of our weekly appearances on *The Andy Williams Show,* the bullies never left me alone. One day I was outside at recess playing baseball with my friends when three boys marched up to me and said, "Hey, Osmond, we're going to beat you up after school." As they walked off laughing, my heart jumped to my throat. What in the world had I done to make someone mad at me?

I was running to get the teacher when a friend named Rocky stopped me and asked what the matter was. When I told him what had happened he merely nodded and said, "Don't worry, they're just trying to scare you." Well, it worked.

As soon as the final bell rang, I high-tailed it out of there. Looking back, I saw those three bullies heading my way. There was nothing to do but run, my heart hammering in my chest. They ran right after me. When the street made a hard left, I stopped just around the corner, determined to stand my ground. Praying for superhuman strength, I took a deep breath and started to sweat. My energy was up, ready for the fight of my life. Poised, I waited for those kids to come barreling around the corner. I waited, but they never came. Scratching my head, I picked up my schoolbooks and headed home.

The next day at school I was surprised to see the three boys who had threatened to beat me up walk into the classroom bruised and bandaged. I looked at Rocky and he smiled.

All those altercations could have been the reason we held regular family boxing matches. We'd pull on our colored boxers, head to the back yard, hang ropes in a square for the boxing ring and then go to it. I held my own, but not for long. My older brothers eventually beat the pulp out of me, but it was good practice.

Even though we practiced defending ourselves, we were taught to run away from fights to avoid getting hurt because of our performing schedule. One day Wayne was coming home from school when a guy came up to him saying, "Hello, Osmond. Do you want to fight?" When Wayne declined, the boy produced a hatpin about eight inches long and rammed it into Wayne's behind!

Another time, in fourth grade, I was walking home from school and noticed a bunch of kids apparently having a lot of fun pounding on a smaller kid. I didn't want to get too close for fear of getting involved somehow. Then somebody came up to me and said, "Hey, that's your brother!" A cold feeling coursed through my body. An overpowering love for my little brother filled me with a strength and courage I didn't know I had. I ran toward the group of kids, grabbed the one on top of Donny by the shirt and pants and threw him into a chain link fence. I walked Donny home, my hand on his shoulder. He cried all the way.

Deep down we know that as children of God we should be treated with respect. Whatever it is—a sneer, an insult, a

shove—it doesn't take much to trigger that elemental feeling of injustice. The saddest thing is when we become so
victimized that we lose our instincts. We may even take
upon ourselves that victim mentality, eventually coming to
believe we deserve the abuse. Maybe we all need to set up a
mental boxing ring to practice fighting off those feelings.
Our Father in Heaven wants us to be aware of our true
worth aside from how anyone on this earth treats us.

I remember one girl, named Nancy, who came to get my
autograph one day. She was visibly shaking in anticipation
of meeting an Osmond. We had a long visit. She was deeply
interested in our close-knit family. It turned out that she
came from a broken home. She had an abusive father, an
alcoholic mother, and a brother in prison for drug dealing.

During our chat, it became apparent that Nancy had
feelings of low self-worth due to her difficult family situation. She believed her entire life would be filled with
heartache and pain. Her only respite was the temporary
peace and happiness she found listening to our records and
dwelling on the idyllic image of our family.

I gathered my courage and asked, "Nancy, do you feel
important to God?"

"Me? No way!" she replied.

"Do you know you are here on earth for a purpose?" I
asked.

"I don't know," she answered.

I explained to Nancy that she was a cherished daughter
of a Heavenly Father, that He loved her, had a plan for her,

and needed her to feel His love today. She broke down, tears flowing.

I hope and pray that Nancy and many others I have had the privilege of visiting with over the years take the opportunity to use their agency to change such distorted thinking. Only as individuals can we make that shift in our thoughts. Though some of us may need professional help to get started on the path to healing and forgiveness, we can begin today to change our ideas about our true worth.

Our great value as human beings is a given regardless of how others treat us. When people treat us less than we deserve in any way, they are unwittingly telling us a great deal about themselves and their own feelings of worth. It's all about them, not us. Our job is to make progress toward recognizing this. Instead of taking the abuse personally, we can find out how to take care of ourselves. Ultimately—and this may be the hardest part—we can pray to feel nothing but love for those doing us wrong. After all, God loves all His children perfectly. Those who treat others unkindly have merely forgotten who they are.

Pop Hysteria

P R A I S E

Journal, age 20

Thousands of fans have surrounded our hotel in London. Scotland Yard ordered the fire department to use fire hoses to blow people out of the street. They did it, too. BBC has a documentary crew outside getting it all on film.

We were just informed that ten to fifteen kids have started to scale the outside of the hotel so they can get access to our window. Three bobbies have been hit over the head with bottles and a fireman was stabbed with a knife. Rough crowd! There is no way to go outside the hotel. I guess it's pizza and home movies for us.

In the early 1970s, The Osmonds were an international pop music sensation, selling 70 million records. Though in the above journal entry I may sound matter-of-fact about young people being sprayed with fire hoses and firemen getting stabbed, bizarre events such as these never ceased to

amaze me. Ironically, while we couldn't help enjoying success, the dangerous mob hysteria that came with it was out
of our control.

England was where all the groups had to be tested. If
the audiences didn't like you there, they'd let you know real
fast. We had concentrated on recording several records
before we went overseas, so we had some hits, but we had
no idea of our real popularity until we got there.

Landing in London, we were astonished to see ten
thousand fans waiting to meet us. From the air they looked
like a teeming hill of ants. As we got off the plane and began
waving, the crowd went crazy. Just then, the balconies they
were standing on began to collapse. We watched, horrified,
as people fell two and three stories. The police escorted us
out of there fast. Six people had been injured at the airport,
and that was just the beginning.

We made the front page news every day for weeks.
Crowds outside our hotel chanted, "We want the
Osmonds," twenty-four hours a day. Girls tried everything
to get closer to us, breaking down hotel doors with axes,
climbing bannisters, and lowering ropes from the roof to
our windows.

For safety reasons, hotels usually reserved an entire
floor for us, while the police scheduled special public
appearances. At certain times, we'd come out on the balcony or landing and wave at the crowd. One day they
neglected to have the cars on the street outside stopped
before someone gave us the go-ahead. As we stepped out

onto the balcony, we saw girls jumping on top of cars as they frantically crossed the street, denting in roofs and hoods. I winced as I witnessed a Rolls Royce get totally demolished.

Because of the mobs of fans, we concocted different ways of camouflaging our entrances and exits. We rode in ambulances, telephone repair vans, paddy wagons, anything to keep from getting noticed. Once I dressed as a bobbie and left the building by way of the fire escape. I only got a block away before I was detected. I raced back to the ladder fast, chased by a mob the whole way.

Subsequent trips to England were as hectic as the first. One time, as our plane descended into Heathrow Airport, the tower asked, "Are the Osmonds on board?" Answering in the affirmative, the pilot was dismayed to find his landing privileges denied. Being rerouted to the Manchester Airport must have really annoyed the other passengers. This was one reason we later traveled in our own private plane.

When we landed in Manchester we still had problems. We looked out the window to see a man-made aisle cutting through a mob of fans; two lines of bobbies stood arm-to-arm from the plane to a private train. The fans again proved more determined and ingenious than the police thought. They were there as we exited the train in a remote section of London and watched as we climbed into our limousines escorted by unmarked police cars. Hundreds bombarded the cars. One girl was thrown over the top of our limo, landing on her back, and was thought to be hit by the car behind us. Upset, we begged to stop the car and take care of her but were told by the police to keep moving. Move we did, but the fans still outsmarted us. On every London corner there were girls posted who signaled each other as our cars went by. In a matter of minutes, they knew where we were staying, a piece of information Scotland Yard had taken great pains to keep quiet.

Performances in those peak years were always pandemonium. One concert I especially remember was in Manchester, England. A bigger crowd had gathered outside the hall than was packed inside. Bobbies stood on the streets yelling at the fans to go away — that there were no more tickets. Inside the sold-out hall the audience pushed forward to get to the front of the stage. We arrived in a bread truck, hoping to get into the concert hall safely.

It was time to go on. As per our usual entrance, the stage was blacked out. There went the count down, we ran on the stage, the lights came up, we spun around, and started to play our opening number. We quickly found the level of screaming so loud, we had to turn our amplifiers to warp level and push our monitors to feedback limits. As a result, we couldn't hear a note we were singing. All we could do was look at each other and laugh, continue to vamp, play the same chord structure over and over, and try to communicate where we were in the song. Just the sight of the audience was enough to blow us away. It looked like a night sky jammed with the grand finale of a fireworks show; thousands and thousands of cameras flashed nonstop for an hour and a half. I think we only played one song that whole night. We halted the show twice, left the stage and came back, all in a disconcerting series of starts and stops.

The audience closest to us often presented more reasons for having to start and stop the show. We often had to deal with what we called pass out lines. The front girls would get pushed forward by the crowd behind them until they either fainted from the excitement or had the wind knocked out of them from being crushed against the stage. Over and over, we had to stop singing and wait while they were retrieved and carried out.

Another regular hold-up occurred when fans tried to climb up on the stage and grab us, and this concert was no exception. The police couldn't figure out how people suddenly appeared on the stage during the show until somebody finally did some investigation. It was discovered that the night before the concert, fans had sneaked into the auditorium, climbed up high in the scaffolding, and hidden there until the show started.

Many people wish for stardom, praise, admiration, and to receive special treatment and attention. There is, however, a great snag in the fabric of worldly fame. Any measure of adulation, acclaim, or applause can be a dangerous distraction for us human beings. How quickly it can turn our heads and fill our hearts. And how quickly it can evaporate.

The pop music business is a great example of the fleeting and addicting nature of fame. Stars can be on top of the world one day and all but forgotten the next. Even at our most popular, we may become so dependent on evidences of approval from others that soon it is never enough, like any addiction. Whether we stay on top and continually long to get higher, or inevitably begin to lose favor in the eyes of the world, acceptance from others is an unreliable source for good feelings about ourselves.

Looks, talents, accomplishments, awards, and honors have nothing to do with our value, although you wouldn't know it from all the attention we humans shower on each other. Just as rejection from others is an undependable source for our feelings of worth, so is acceptance. Neither rejection nor acceptance have anything to do with our true, intrinsic worth as children of God.

From fans screaming our name to a friend paying us a casual compliment, these things tell us more about others than about ourselves. These expressions are merely evidences of others' feelings — what is going on in their minds and hearts at that moment — the motives for which we may not accurately know. We can be outwardly gracious because of this outward sharing, but inwardly, we can immediately give our Father in Heaven all the credit. I guarantee the constant warmth of divine acceptance blasts temporary worldly praise right out of the grandstand.

Above and beyond all earthly considerations, we are His. Every breath we take, everything we do and have are all His gifts to us. Whenever I receive any degree of praise, I try to say a silent prayer. Rather than personalizing the compliment, I thank my Heavenly Father for the opportunity to connect with others, for insight into their hearts, for the chance to be an instrument in His hands. By thinking this way, I am not only drawing closer to God, but I am arming myself with a powerful protection against having my feelings of worth fluctuate up and down like pop songs on a chart. God's love is the most steady source of all applause. He cheers for us continuously. Such a subtle change in our hearts can make such a great difference.

Many fellow entertainers I've met through the years seem to scramble in every way possible to stay poised on the cutting edge. I've watched dear friends in this extremely unpredictable business fall from grace without any spiritual net to catch them. When the awards and gold records materialized, my brothers and I were grateful, but deep down we knew fame was a fickle, fleeting thing.

Journal, age 20

Now we're in France. The concert was crazy. When we got here we didn't know what to expect. We were told the records are just as big here, only the French people have no image of the Osmond Brothers because there are no teen magazines showing pictures of us. One guy tipped us off by saying, "You're going to have a really hippie-looking audience." We thought that was strange.

Well, he was right. How we can have such a different following while singing the same songs is totally amazing. The crowd was jammed, drugs everywhere, long-haired people freaking out all over the place. We were really scared. We changed the show drastically. No "Sweet and Innocent" type numbers, only the heavy rock songs and a lot of vamping. Well, it went off well. I couldn't believe it. Totally black and white difference!

Variables like these didn't throw us like they might have. Though I've come a long way since then in my understanding of God's love for me, I believe even in those early days, my family's ultimate reliance on a power greater than ourselves helped keep us relatively grounded, especially when we were caught up in that whirlwind of dizzying fame. We always felt the basic need to turn to our Heavenly Father for guidance. Our ears were tuned in to something more lasting than applause, our eyes opened to something beyond the spotlight. But even the most down-to-earth are not immune to some type of flying debris.

Sound Check

PRAYER

It was early summer, 1971. I had just turned 18 years old. Behind me were 14 years of the discipline and structure of a successful show business lifestyle: demanding rehearsals, relentless schedules, endless public appearances, and mounting pressure to meet performance expectations.

My brothers and I had recently exploded into the mainstream pop market. We had just returned from a successful trip to Japan which was followed immediately by a concert tour to Ohio and Texas. These appearances were designed to determine how our newest songs would be accepted by the public. "One Bad Apple" was gold; it had hit number one on the charts and had stayed there for five weeks. Preparations were being made for yet another tour, nationwide. After selling millions of records, we were soon named Top New Group of the Year by all three pop music magazines. The trips all over the world, international exposure, media acclaim, and the constant talk of greater things to come were more than we had ever dreamed.

But I was tired. At eighteen, I felt as tired as an old man. Home at last, at least for a few weeks, I was oblivious to the early summer day along Utah's Wasatch Front. The sun was just beginning to melt away the snowy mountain caps, exposing the new green of pines and aspens. Living close by Brigham Young University, I had no notion of how most kids my age were feeling, of the students' relief of a completed semester, or of the atmosphere changing from studies and snow skiing to summer jobs and water skiing. The anticipation of a new season here at home was totally lost on me, as foreign and far away as Japan. The brief lull between tours felt like a silent, eerie eye in the center of my cyclonic existence. I suddenly felt I was missing something essential.

I slowly maneuvered the family's gold Cadillac through the quiet Provo streets toward the canyon road. My mind was numb, dead as a stage after a concert. No comforting, practical thoughts came to help explain what I was feeling. I had to get away, be by myself, and try to make some sense of my life.

Against this stifling silence in my head arose confusing emotions from my gut that seemed to turn me inside out. Helplessness, despair, and pain seared through me like a blinding hot spotlight. What was happening to me? Why had I lost the focus of my well-planned, perfectly laid out life? And why had I picked up a butcher knife from the kitchen on my way out to the car?

The knife lay beside me on the car seat though I hadn't

consciously intended to bring it. Perhaps it represented a way out, a solid option symbolizing a release from misery should I lose the battle.

I drove through neighborhoods, tears streaming down my face. Incredibly, I passed people pleasantly going about their day. Couples walked along the sidewalks talking and laughing. Families loaded up their campers getting ready for their vacations. A man knelt in his front yard planting bright flowers.

When I arrived at the base of the mountain, I saw guys on motorcycles racing in figure eights as if all the world belonged to them. I thought to myself, what would it be like? How would it feel to spend time just having fun, being with friends, playing sports, attending school, or going fishing with Father? What was it like to date, to go to dances, or to talk about teenage things with other teenagers? It occurred to me that I had never experienced any of those things, though I knew they existed. I had recently seen the movie *American Graffiti* and couldn't relate to one bit of it.

Here I was, part of a loving family, successful in a professional career before I was twenty years old, a bright future apparently in store, and not a reason in the world to feel such despair. Despite all of this, there it was—despair so thick the sunny day appeared gray, clouded, closing in. I felt trapped like an insect under glass. The whole world seemed to be peering down at me as if through a microscope. Clinging to this distorted perception, I pitied myself for being who I was, lonely and singled out.

Having been taught to pray since before I could put two words together, I began to cry out loud to my Heavenly Father. Perhaps if I talked to Him, if I poured out all my frustrations and misery, He would give me answers. A short way into the canyon, I couldn't drive any further. I needed to completely concentrate on my prayer. Parking the car beside the road, I began climbing up the mountain through the trees and brush looking for a secluded place where I could think and pray.

Finding a big pine tree with a patch of grass underneath it, I fell to my knees. Just as I began to pray, I heard someone coming up a pathway nearby. It was a young couple, probably BYU students, laughing and being silly. Startled from what I felt was a sacred moment, I jumped to my feet and headed back to the car feeling first embarrassed and agitated, then downright annoyed. Even in my desperate need to be alone, people intruded. How was I to find myself and feel whole if I could never find the time or place to be alone? I felt owned by the world, pressed, packaged, and purchased like one of our albums sold in every record store.

Why me, I wondered. Everybody else seemed so happy, holding hands as they climbed a hill, making noise on motorcycles, piling in the family camper. Self-pity built up inside me as I got back in the car and drove off in search of another secluded spot. I came to a bluff overlooking the city, parked, and got out of the car. There seemed to be nobody around, but even in this lonely place, inner darkness crowded in on me. Its silent push and crush was as real as any mob of screaming fans.

I thought for a few minutes before attempting to find just the right words to say that would explain my confused unhappiness to my Heavenly Father. I told Him I felt helpless and trapped, that I had never felt such depression and misery. Even as I spoke, I felt guilty for indulging in these ungrateful feelings in the middle of my family's success.

As I prayed, I unconsciously reached for the knife I had brought lying beside me in the dirt. This prayer wasn't working. As I poured out my heart, listing my woes, I only felt myself drifting farther into an ocean of depression. I wanted out—not out of show business, but out of life. It seemed the only way to solve my inexplicable problems. I watched as my hands lifted the knife to my throat. With tears streaming down my face, I cried to an unseen power for help, for some acknowledgement that God was hearing me, for some relief from the drenching darkness.

To think where he's been, the world he has seen
Would baffle the wise for a time,
But snap goes the string, the dollies will fall,
The teacher uncovers the crime.
He's swimming in tears, he's too far from shore,
He's drowning with nowhere to go.
"Don't think. It's okay," doesn't work for him now;
There isn't a stage or a show.

— Merrill Osmond, "Wind Up the Dolls," 1985

This was the real thing, my friends, life in one of its deepest abysses, at least as deep as it could get for this particular 18-year-old. At times like these it may seem as if we're drowning, but in reality, this is right where God wants us. In His own mysterious way, he had my attention.

What happened next was not at all earthshaking. Sitting there on that silent bluff I heard no words, I saw no one. There was only a sense of warmth. It came to me in a soft breeze lifting my hair, in the rays of the sun on my face, and in a sensation of soothing, encircling arms. A fresh, spiritual strength passed into my soul from heaven's embrace, filling me with what I now recognize as perfect love—a love so pure that it stands on its own, completely above my failings and completely beyond my successes.

As the darkness lifted, I experienced a feeling of safety and well-being I never felt before, as if miraculously lifted out of danger by an unseen rescuer. I stayed there for a long time, doing nothing, just contemplating these feelings.

Finally, I picked myself up, got in the car and drove away from the bluff, back to the family I loved, back to my responsibilities. Outwardly, nothing had changed. Inwardly, everything had changed. Now I sensed a new capacity to handle my life just as it was, with all its challenges, and to perform to the best of my ability as long as required.

Just as the secure foundations of my life seemed to turn to sand, I felt a new spiritual base forming. It rose out of the simple fact that my Heavenly Father was watching over me.

Though my life would probably never be normal, He loved me. He cared. There was a safe place to turn. And that place was just a prayer away.

> *Then out of the blue come a few with bright oars*
> *Moving quickly with no time to lose,*
> *Gathering bits at a time, leaving nothing behind*
> *As each movement they purposely choose.*
> *He watched as they cleaned both outside and in,*
> *Caressing each part as they mended,*
> *Correcting each flaw with precision and love,*
> *A vision I did not want ended.*
> — Merrill Osmond, "Wind Up the Dolls," 1985

No matter what our situation, that gathering up of our broken pieces, that cleansing and caressing, that correcting of our hearts and minds is mercifully available to us all. Every time we feel overwhelmed, I believe it's simply because we aren't tuning in to God's love. If we exercise our agency to listen, He sends his warmth and love to sustain us through His state-of-the-art spiritual sound system. Unlike an ear-blasting amplifier at a rock concert, His is most often so quiet we have to fine tune our souls to hear it.

When we do hear it, it is essential to note that any heavenly communication is a gift above and beyond our own efforts, a blessing we do not earn, an act of divine grace. Though our efforts range from weak to mighty, we must give all the credit and glory to God alone.

It's exciting to discover new ways to more effectively tap into that heavenly amplifier. I find if I do nothing but vent all my injuries, injustices, and infirmities to my Father in Heaven, I am only cementing them in my mind. Though I wish to briefly rehearse my troubles, of which He is already mindful, I try to spend most of my praying time conversing with my Father about how He feels about me, His unconditional love, my great value to Him, His watchful care over me, His plan for me, and what He would have me do.

It felt strange and unfamiliar at first to pray about my great worth. But as I continue to do it, more often than not the divine spirit of truth confirms the accuracy of the things I am praying about. If I am in tune, it is unmistakable. It comes in a feeling of well-being, of warmth, and of confidence.

Spiritual affirmations are so much more powerful than the personal affirmations we hear so much about today. Though our troubles may not change, God will work a miracle in us. We'll take courage, get ideas, and better cope with our situation when we begin to hear, however faintly at first, the divine melody of His love.

𝓘𝓶𝓪𝓰𝓮

TRUTH

Journal, age 18

We performed in Japan today. It was a little bit embarrassing. There was this Japanese guy who put us all in a little car and held his bull horn out the window screaming, "Come see the Osmonds! They're groovy!" They took us to a restaurant tonight and served us jellyfish tentacles, stuffed pig, and some kind of animal brains. Father got mad at me 'cause I only had the orange drink.

I guess because I have a round face the Japanese girls relate to me. There was this certain girl in the crowd today who caught my eye. So many people were pushing, I didn't really have a chance to say hi but out of the blue she yelled, "Please marry me!" Then she reached over to hand me a ring that looked like it had three good-sized diamonds and some pearls on it. Just then one of our bodyguards hit her hand and that beautiful ring flew up in the air and was lost.

It's crazy, isn't it? This girl got the idea in her head to marry me going on my public image alone. But people are so much more complicated than what we see on the outside.

I remember the one bathroom in our Ogden house with its pink fixtures and clawfoot tub. It was so rare to find a place to be alone in our house. As a little guy, I loved to lock the door of that bathroom and look at my face in the mirror, thinking if I stared long enough I'd see through to my real self. Too soon, I was interrupted by banging on the door. I'd have to get out fast or get into trouble with whoever needed the bathroom.

Being on stage did not come naturally for me. I was a rather shy kid filled with my share of doubts and fears. I was given the nickname Bucky Boy at school because my teeth stuck out a bit. In addition, I was the only blond in the family, relatively speaking, until Jimmy came along. People would tease me saying, "Are you sure you didn't get mixed up in the hospital?" That stuck with me. Could I be someone else's kid?

Childish insecurities like these are common to most kids, but mine were complicated by show business. I wasn't just a kid performing live in front of thousands of people; I was a chubby kid performing live in front of thousands of people. At least that's what everyone told me.

I was told I needed to be thinner because of the image thought necessary for our success. I wasn't quite as slender as my brothers, which didn't look good on stage or TV. Starting at an early age, I was constantly monitored and told what I could and couldn't eat. I would often leave the table before I was satisfied so I wouldn't be tempted to eat any more. Throughout my youth my father glared at me if I ordered something from a menu at a restaurant that was incompatible with my diet. It was especially difficult watching my brothers order whatever they wanted, salivating as they gulped down unlimited helpings of hamburgers, french fries, and milk shakes.

The idea that TV cameras add ten pounds didn't help either. People in the industry who were involved in our career teased me lightheartedly about being the chunky one, but it wasn't a joke to me. As I got older and we entered the pop music market, there was continual TV coverage of the Osmonds along with our photos appearing in endless teen magazines. All this exposure added to the pressure I felt.

I was inundated with mixed messages. My family and managers depended on me to do whatever it took to appear slim and appealing, reminding me regularly to watch my weight. At the same time, fan mail poured in from admiring girls all over the world declaring how good-looking and desirable I was. Sad to say, the negative input won out.

I was a young teen when a well-meaning but mis-informed person in the industry taught me how to throw up after eating. In those days the eating disorder now referred to as bulimia was not common knowledge, but we did something similar. We would "soda out," which consisted of drinking a baking soda solution after eating to induce vomiting. Sad to say, I participated in this for many years, even after I was married. My wife Mary finally convinced me how unwise this was and extracted from me a promise to quit. It amazes me now to what extremes I went to keep up the physical image I felt compelled to portray.

Why is it that we go to such lengths to appear a certain way to the world? Where along the way did that illusive diamond ring, that true value of our sparkling souls, get knocked out of an outstretched hand, fly up in the air, and disappear?

Eating disorders, fad dieting, cosmetic surgeries, excessive body building and exercise, extreme clothing, hair, jewelry, makeup, tattoos, and piercings are all about how we appear in the mirror and to others. They are about making a splash, feeling important, generating comparisons. Once we get started on an exaggerated concern for personal appearance we are in danger of making it a major reason for enjoying life, or despising it.

Evidently, there is something missing in our inner lives that causes us to expend such a great deal of our resources on our outer selves. It's all about what is going on in our heads. For a myriad of reasons, we decide that certain things determine our feelings of worth: our shape, our weight, our youthfulness, our hair, our clothes, our uniqueness. If we decide these things are unacceptable, we search for ways to improve or accentuate them. We may buy a new outfit, work out at the gym, try a new diet, or suffer through expensive cosmetic surgery, all to feel acceptable, attractive, worthwhile, validated.

How long do the feelings of high self-worth that come

with these worldly solutions last? Clothes go out of style, bodies tire, weight fluctuates, skin ages. No amount of effort or money can ensure endless youth, boundless energy, and flawless beauty. If we depend on these things for our sense of identity, our feelings about ourselves will fluctuate like the needle on the scale as we hop on and off.

How then, can we tap into a nice steady stream of good feelings about ourselves no matter what the scale says on any given day, no matter whether we get our exercise in, no matter if our clothes are the latest trend? We can feel good about ourselves by holding truth in our minds. Harmful lies so easily sneak in. I'm reminded of a curious story.

We were on tour in Sweden when I was 14. It was around 3:00 in the morning when I felt a bump at the foot of my hotel room bed. My eyes popped opened. Staring into the darkness, I saw two shadows of little people traipsing around the room. What were they doing, going through my pants pockets? I shook my head trying to wake up, hoping it was all a dream. The midgets continued rummaging through my things. I decided to do something about it. Darting toward one of the culprits, I caught him by the leg and rolled him onto the floor, yelling and screaming, "Stop, you little jerk!" While I held on to the character for dear life, the other one ran to the window and escaped. It took all my strength to subdue the remaining thief until the police came.

Lies can be like trained burglars, sometimes small enough to sneak into our minds unnoticed, doing their dirty work under the cover of darkness. It's up to us to turn on the lights, recognize them for what they are, wrestle them to the ground, and send them packing.

When I was a little boy, I childishly wondered if I were someone else's kid. The truth is, I was. I was a child of a Heavenly Father who loved me as much as He loved my older, smarter, slimmer brothers and as much as he loved my younger, more adorable siblings.

We will enjoy continual high feelings of worth if we focus our thoughts on eternal truths rather than on what we're told by others or by searching out temporary fixes. The worth of our individual souls is beyond our comprehension. Our value is a given. It stands apart from our weight, shape, clothes, or any other aspect of our physical appearance.

Though some may need professional help in overcoming disorders associated with a false self-image, we can make great progress on our own by recognizing any distorted thinking and correcting it. I've found that the best way to do this is through prayer. By praying about truths — who we are, and our great value to God apart from our outward appearance and what others think or say — we exercise our spiritual muscles and access a power greater than our own. If we persist, we'll come to know that what we're praying about is true. Our feelings of self-worth will soar to heights we never imagined and will remain steady. As a result, we'll treat ourselves with the respect we deserve and consequently truly look and feel better without excesses of any kind.

Performance

PERFECTION

As is customary, I was baptized a member of The Church of Jesus Christ of Latter-day Saints when I turned eight years old. My parents gave me a lot of attention as this important event approached, carefully instructing me in the meaning of this sacred ordinance.

When the big day came, I was filled with apprehension. After arriving at the church building, I put on my spotlessly white baptismal clothing: a shirt and pair of pants. My father, who was to perform the baptism, was also dressed in white. He stood tall beside me, his big hand on my shoulder. Together we stepped down the few steps into the bathtub-warm baptismal font. With my family gathered to watch, I was totally immersed in the chest-deep water and lifted up, blinking and dripping, a thrill of gratitude surging through my small body. I felt completely pure and full of God's love.

Later, kneeling beside my bed, I prayed fervently to keep that feeling. I told my brothers and friends that I was washed clean and would never, ever make one single mistake that would tarnish the shine on my soul. I was sure I would see my Heavenly Father's face again someday if I could just keep from sin. Every day I bounced around in a sparkling bubble of perfection. The very idea that I would ever sin was like a sharp pinpoint threatening to burst my bubble. I promised myself that I just wouldn't allow it. I would be perfect from that day on.

Well, of course it wasn't long before I slipped up. One day I was playing a game of cops and robbers outside with my brother. I was the patrolman and Wayne was the robber. As he came riding his bike down the street, I held up my hand to stop him, but he didn't stop. This made me a little mad, so I picked up a stick and waited. When Wayne sped by again, I stuck the willow in his spokes. The bike flipped in the air and my brother with it, smashing up right before my eyes. Hearing Wayne's screams, Father came running and, learning what had happened, gave me a sound spanking.

That wasn't nearly the worst of it. My smarting seat was nothing compared to the ache in my heart. I had really done it now. In a moment of weakness I had broken my baptismal covenant once and for all. I had failed God. My plans for a sinless life went up in smoke. Now I had an ugly black mark on my heavenly chart. In an instant I had completely forfeited my chance at perfection. I was shattered.

To me, all seemed lost. But my father had something up his sleeve. After the spanking he took me in his arms speaking words of love and forgiveness and hope, showing me how, even in the face of this damning evidence, I could be clean once more. In this emotion-packed moment, he introduced me to the magical atonement of Jesus Christ. What an impact it had on me! I would spend the rest of my life applying this glorious, liberating truth.

The bad news is we will all make mistakes. We all sin to some degree. Try as we might, there is no way around this reality. Remember, we agreed to come to earth to learn from our own experience. The good news is we have a Savior. When we become aware of an error, no matter how slight, all we have to do is turn our thoughts to the Lord and feel His arms around us, much as I felt my earthly father's loving embrace. Once we feel this love, we will more readily pick ourselves up, dust ourselves off, and press forward with renewed determination to do what is right and good.

A problem occurs when we continually condemn ourselves for our wrong choices, mistakes, sins, even our innocent human errors. Because of my history I have always struggled with this crippling perfectionism.

When I was just a little guy, my father critiqued our rehearsals. He insisted we practice until we had our notes, our steps, and even our facial expressions flawlessly synchronized. If a rehearsal went long, Father often turned it over to Alan who then became the disciplinarian. We worked ourselves until a routine was perfect. It became the norm. On *The Andy Williams Show* we were dubbed the One-Take Osmonds, nailing our routines on the first try.

I must have been just eight or nine when Andy Williams asked us to say a few lines on the show. Since all we'd ever done was sing and dance, we couldn't believe we had a chance to read a cue card. We practiced all week. I had just one line to say but it was rather tricky. Boy, did I work hard on it.

Then, during a rehearsal Andy said, "To make it look better, we're going to take the cue cards away so you won't be reading them." After that I got nervous. I sweated, I lost sleep, I even had nightmares over that line, thinking I would blow it somehow with millions of people watching me.

Showtime came and we sang our opening song. Andy came down and sat with us on the steps. It was time for me to say my line which was, *When he first put his pants on, he tucked his tails into his pants like a shirt.*

In my head I was repeating it over and over so I would not forget it. All of a sudden the red signal light came on. I stared into it and went completely blank. I started to mumble, "When he first put his tails on, he tucked his pants into his shirt like a . . . " The audience laughed. Andy went white. He looked down at me and said, "You mean he tucked his tails into his pants like a shirt?"

"Yes, that's what I wanted to say," I said. The audience laughed again. My face burned. It sure wasn't funny to me.

Much of my life has been spent in front of an audience. Every time I enter a stage, or other forum, it doesn't take long to size up the type of crowd I'm up against. Some audiences are responsive, easily entertained, reflecting energy back. Others are there to find fault, scrutinizing every move for some imperfection, which makes for a long night. But regardless of the type of audience, they are all made up of people who paid money to see a professional performance. As a result of this midset, in any area of my life — as a husband, father, neighbor, church worker, producer, or businessman — when I don't perform up to my own expectations I have a tendency to be very hard on myself.

I am prone to think of life itself as a performance, overly concerning myself with expectations and working too hard to be a people pleaser. The show business saying, *keep 'em happy,* was ingrained in my brain early on. But in applying this philosophy, I judge myself much too harshly. I give myself a sound mental spanking for what I consider my failings, over and over again, but for what reason? Does punishing myself rid me of guilt? Have I been trying to save myself?

Well, I have found self-condemnation to be totally ineffective. It gets me nowhere in my self-improvement efforts and I imagine it isn't working for you either. We condemn and punish, condemn and punish, like riding on a hellish roller coaster that never stops. Remaining on this jerking, jolting track keeps us from being still and feeling that divine outpouring of love.

All this stressing out and judging and punishing and saving ourselves is denying us of Christ's gift of power and grace. He didn't come to earth because some of us need a Savior, he came because all of us need a Savior. Only through him can we be whole. It's better to perform, sure and steady, out of gratitude for a patient, accepting God who loves us despite our imperfections. God is not nearly as hard on us as some of us are on ourselves. Through the merits of His Son, He will accept our every pure-hearted effort and will send light and comfort in our failures.

Throughout my life I've penned long personal to-do lists, not just itemizing daily chores such as getting the car serviced or taking out the garbage, but enumerating lofty goals for personal improvement in every area of my life. I wrote this one in 1994:

1. Get out of Debt – Put your faith in God.
2. Find yourself again – What do you want?
3. Put your Marriage in Shape.
4. Put Supplies in place / all Storageable Items.
5. Health Concerns dealt with. / Diet, Exercise.
6. Find income.
7. Enjoy the outdoors with the Family.
8. Go to Church and Bear Testimony often.
9. assess all undone relationships that Need attention.
10. Read & write daily.
11. attend the Temple often.
12. Live Every Commandment
13. Relax and Smell the Roses.
14. Paint

The funny thing is, if we had all our wits about us in a given moment and could make a truly comprehensive list of everything we should do to be perfect, it would be a mile long—a list to end all lists. Perhaps we would then see how discouraging and impossible a task we are setting up for ourselves. Too often our sense of well-being depends on checking off items on our perfection list. What if there aren't enough check marks? How do we feel then? The sickness of perfectionism arises when we feel the need to perform just so we can feel okay about ourselves.

Don't get me wrong. There's nothing inherently wrong with to-do lists. It all depends on how we feel about them and why we're accomplishing all the listed items. I used to say something like, "If I can just get the things on this list done, I'll finally feel good about myself." Now I say, "Here's another of my to-do lists. I'll tackle each item as I feel inspired and do it out of my love for Heavenly Father." In this way I use my list not only to get things done but to draw closer to God and feel His love.

God's love doesn't fluctuate according to our accomplishments. We can learn to feel His love apart from our performance. He doesn't expect or require perfection from us at this time during our earthly experience. Instead, He rejoices in our progress. Only God Himself is perfectly patient, perfectly understanding, perfectly accepting of us whether we lie in bed all day doing nothing or get up with the sun and work our heads off, checking everything off our list.

Of course, God wishes us to improve and do much good. What works best for me, along with my inevitable to-do list, is simply a prayer. I wake up each morning, roll out of bed onto my knees, and ask Heavenly Father what He would have me do that day. I don't usually get a news flash, but I do usually feel His encouragement. Armed with this love, I then go forward with what feels right, doing all things out of love for Him.

When I feel I'm not quite measuring up in some task, I try to remember to turn to God. When I do, I feel my Savior's power making up for my failings and giving me new ideas. The amazing twist is that in surrendering my perfectionism to God's love, I actually perform more effectively. I have more energy, I feel more positive, and I don't mind so much what others may think. I don't impose undue pressure on myself, and I don't stress out.

The hardest and most important work we can do is within our own hearts, but be aware. We can't even do this ridding-ourselves-of-perfectionism thing perfectly! Perhaps those of us who are especially hard on ourselves need only one item on our to-do list: Feel God's love. The idea is to make progress. If we can feel God's love in place of our desire to be perfect even for a moment, and the rest of the day we stress out, we've made progress. If we persist in turning to God, those moments of peace will soon lengthen.

Gold Record

WORTH

At the back of our property in Ogden was a canal. On the other side of the canal was a chain link fence separating us from a reform school for wayward kids. As a small boy, the idea of dangerous characters living so close to us caused me a great deal of uneasiness. Every morning as I went outside to do my chores, I walked out into the pasture, staring fascinated through the trees into the yard of this school. I watched some of the boys walking from building to building. Others stopped to stare back at me not moving a muscle. How did somebody end up in a place like that? Where were their families? What had they done that they had to be kept separate from regular people? I imagined that if one of them escaped, they'd probably beat the daylights out of me.

One day Donny, Jay, and I were playing in the orchard when suddenly two boys dressed in reform school uniforms ran by. Seeing us playing in the dirt, one said to the other, "Let's get 'em." The one who spoke started toward us, but the other kid stopped him.

"No, let's get out of here," he said.

Terrified, we ran into the house and told Mother. She immediately called the school and in five minutes our yard was swarming with uniformed guards. Sirens and whistles echoed through the town. About an hour later we saw the boys hauled away in handcuffs, their clothes torn and dirty, their faces bloodied.

Another time I was flying a brand new kite in the pasture. Horrified, I watched as the wind blew it across the canal and into a tree next to the reform school boundary. To get my kite, I'd have to cross the canal bridge and get right up close to that chain link fence. Slowly, one step at a time, I made my way toward the downed kite. Once at the fence, I reached for my kite only to find one of the reform school boys walking toward me. I froze in my shoes. He put his hands on the chain link and said, "Hi." I turned and ran all the way home.

Almost three decades later, I was invited by a friend to speak at the Utah State Prison. This wasn't my first experience of this kind. I had spoken to such groups before and had found those who attended these meetings very well behaved and attentive.

I entered the chapel and found the room full of medium security inmates dressed in prison blue. My friend stepped up to the podium to introduce me. I was surprised as he began relating the story of my fearful childhood experiences living next to a reform school. He then asked one of the inmates seated on the back row to come forward.

This man then explained that he had been one of those boys behind the chain link fence of that Ogden reform school. He used to look into our farmyard and watch us as we worked and played. Someone had told him we were the Osmond kids. He said he had felt so proud to be living in the same town as the Osmonds.

The room fell silent. He approached me. I opened my arms, and we tenderly embraced. This man was no longer a person to be feared. For reasons unknown, he had never been able to cope appropriately with the outside world, but that was none of my concern. He was my brother.

Journal, age 18

Our Security put us in our rooms tonight and locked us up, but I sneaked out. The reason was I saw a girl wearing an Osmond t-shirt and cap sitting all by herself outside my window crying her eyes out. Something told me I needed to go down and see her. I made my way out the back door and into the parking lot without anybody seeing me. As I walked up to her, I saw that she seemed a little bit incoherent. When I said hello she looked at me and started to scream. "No, no," I said. "Don't do that. I just wanted to come out and say hi to you. If you make a lot of noise I'll have to leave." It was then I noticed there were bottles lying around on the ground. She had taken a ton of pills! I ran inside and called our Security. They got an ambulance and took her to the hospital. I'm so grateful I was prompted to go out and see her.

I'm reminded of the story of our song "One Bad Apple." After six years on *The Andy Williams Show*, we put our efforts into finding a new niche. Time after time, our songs went nowhere. One day we were presented with this song and knew immediately it would be a sure hit. Vocal coaches instructed us in the new pop style, which was so different from the barbershop we had been singing all our lives. It became our first big rock and roll single.

Though we worked tirelessly on every one of our songs, some climbed to the top of the charts while others flopped. The pop music industry is extremely trendy; hit songs come and go. The value of human beings, however, is not subject to ratings like the Top Forty on American Bandstand. It makes no difference what we do or what the world thinks when it comes to our value in God's eyes.

We're told that God is no respecter of persons. He loves the convicted rapist or murderer as much as he loves the innocent victim of these horrible crimes. The Savior invites us to value ourselves as he values us, and to value one another the same way. If we could really see each other as Christ sees us, we would treat every person we meet with awe and respect. This doesn't mean we trust all people, but it does mean we try to have nothing but kind and compassionate feelings in our hearts toward them.

In God's bushel basket there are no bad apples. Each one of us is pure gold. Only when we realize this do we begin to shine.

𝕴𝖓𝖐𝖊𝖉

MARRIAGE

Journal, age 19

Oh Heavenly Father, please lead me to the one I can spend my life with, someone who knows and understands the meaning of a forever family. The temptations of the flesh are so great! Help me to keep myself worthy of the wife I'll someday have.

I wrote the above journal entry at a time when my brothers and I were experiencing overwhelming success. Multiple hit records were moving up the charts, sales were in the millions, and concerts were selling out. Along with the fame came a flood of temptations. I was a young man surrounded by thousands of admiring girls in an industry rightly known for its decadent life style. The press practically breathed down our necks, hoping to find a smudge on the spotless Osmond image.

They had no success. My brothers and I had been taught uncompromising sexual purity. My parents' example of total commitment to marriage and faithfulness to each other cemented their teachings. In addition, our religious beliefs that marriage and family were important to personal spiritual progression had a great influence on us.

Having been taught well through example and precept, I looked forward to finding a soul mate. Given my circumstances, I was old for my age. Even at nineteen I felt I should actively seek a wife. My desire to have a family was foremost in my heart and mind.

Of course, none of us Osmond brothers had dated much. Funny how that happened with girls breaking down our door. We were so busy working, performing, and traveling, we didn't have much of a social life. What good was a mob of fans, or even one hysterical girl, for the purpose of serious dating? Obviously, it would be difficult to date a fan club member. Where was I going to find a girl with her feet planted firmly on the ground?

Our managers had their own ideas about our love lives. In order to keep the Osmonds a viable pop group, attractive to the teeny boppers, we needed to remain "available." Because of this mind set, I felt a huge sense of responsibility to my family. We were totally dedicated to and united in our busy career. I sang the lead in most of our songs and everybody relied on me. In addition, Church leaders had specifically expressed their confidence in us as ambassadors. We had a mission to share our faith, however indirectly. Would marriage throw a cog in the works? With all these concerns, I needed God's help in making this decision, if and when I found the girl of my dreams.

About this time, Mary Carlson, an LDS girl from Heber, Utah, was preparing to graduate from Brigham Young University with a degree in business education. Raised for most of her life on a dairy farm by her widowed mother, she had worked her own way through college. As a beauty queen and cheerleader, Mary was not lacking in dating opportunities. However, one day she did an uncharacteristic thing. She accepted a blind date. That date was me. She later wrote in her journal,

> I didn't really want to go out with Merrill Osmond. Even though I had never heard him sing, I knew of the Osmonds, and I figured he'd be stuck up and want to talk about himself all night. So I wasn't all that excited. To tell the truth, I didn't even know which one of the brothers he was. I was nervous about meeting him, but the minute he said, "Hi! Are you Mary?" I knew he was different. We had a fantastic evening and quickly became friends.

Though there were thousands of girls who could recognize me on the street, Mary wasn't one of them. She had ignored all the hoopla surrounding the Osmonds.

Here was that level-headed girl I had prayed for, who also happened to be beautiful, smart, and fun. More importantly, we shared the same religious beliefs and family goals. At the time, my parents happened to be looking for a private tutor for Marie and Jimmy. I suggested Mary. It was easily arranged, and the set-up gave me plenty of opportunities to see her that summer.

Too soon we were off on another concert tour. Being separated from Mary made me realize how much I cared for her. I tracked her down in Hawaii where she was vacationing with her aunt, and we spent a lot of time on the phone. By the time we each had returned home, we were ready to make a commitment. Well, Mary and I were ready, but nobody else was.

When I announced my intention to get married right away, there couldn't have been a bigger shock wave than if I had said I was joining The Jackson Five. Though Virl and Tom were both married, I was the first of the performing brothers to come up with the wild idea. Boy, did I ever make a lot of people nervous. They said things like, "The lead singer of the Osmonds getting married? How could he? It'll destroy the group!" One manager told me in no uncertain terms that marriage would ruin my recording and performing career. He also threw in his opinion that the whole Osmond family would go belly up. Members of my family, especially my father, argued against it. Looking back, I can certainly see their point of view. I was awfully young. But I was determined.

Journal, age 20

Our manager and agent are trying to make me feel like I'm going to ruin everything if I get married. But I've never felt so sure about anything in my life. Mary

is to be my wife, I just know this. There are so many con-
flicting voices. Only my sweet mother stands by me.

While my mother was on our side, Mary's wasn't quite so convinced. When Mary told her mother that she was in love with me, she replied, "Sure, you and thirty thousand other girls!" She was afraid Mary was infatuated with the glamour and glitz of our high-profile lifestyle. It was only after spending some time with us that she saw we were truly in love and accepted me as a son-in-law. My mother-in-law's home, tucked in the Wasatch Mountains, was to become one of my favorite sanctuaries from the world, and a choice fishing spot for me and my sons.

Even amid the opposition, Mary and I were married in the Salt Lake Temple only months after we met. Because of the media hype about the first Osmond brother to get married, we drove to the temple in separate cars to avoid attracting attention. I was disguised in a straw hat and sunglasses, trying my best not to look like a nervous bridegroom.

Even with all these precautions, there was the press to meet us on the temple grounds along with a crowd of curious, noisy people. It was in a quiet, private ceremony inside the temple where we were sealed as one for time and all eternity.

Mary and I were married but, oddly enough, she had never seen me perform in person. She got her first opportunity just after our wedding when we began an engagement in Las Vegas. Mary traveled with us everywhere we went during our first few years of marriage before the children came. She wrote,

> *I was totally shocked when I saw what Merrill did up on that stage. I knew he sang but I had no idea he danced and played the banjo or any of the other instruments. I was amazed. He had never told me about all this!*

No, I hadn't told her much about what I did. I didn't think it mattered. And it didn't. Here was someone who loved me just as I was without all the pressure to perform. What a sweet reward I had waiting for me after performing two shows back to back. While the whole world seemed to bang on the doors and scream at the windows, I'd calmly go up to my suite, order room service, and spend the rest of the evening with my gentle wife who was kind enough to rub my tired feet. I felt sorry for my brothers and hoped they'd find the right girls soon. They were missing out!

Our first home was a little duplex in Provo. I couldn't get over how strange and wonderful it was to come home to a loving wife settled in a small apartment rather than to a whole houseful of rowdy brothers.

Journal, age 20

Father said I'm a little heavy, so I'm going to do something about it. After I came home Mary was in the kitchen making oatmeal cookies. Boy, they were just great!

Journal, age 20

Alan, Wayne, and Jay went to a dance tonight. You know, it really feels weird not being a real part of the guys anymore. But in a way it's sort of neat not having to impress someone all the time.

Marital bliss aside, I quickly foresaw some major adjustments. There was more to marriage than settling into a love nest of quiet, warm companionship.

For twenty years, my every waking moment had been devoted to my family. My days revolved around performances, concerts, tours, and business. I was accustomed to routine, discipline, and precision. In rehearsal, if something didn't turn out to the brothers' unanimous satisfaction, we did it over and over until it did. Whatever it was—a few bars of harmony, a series of dance steps, an instrumental chord progression—it had to be perfected before it was acceptable. Life with Mary was much more spontaneous. Suddenly there was no program, no agenda, no run-through, no script. In this marriage thing, you just had to wing it!

Journal, age 21

Mary had a big test tomorrow so I said I'd clean the kitchen. Boy, I'll never say that again!

I also learned I couldn't just blurt out my thoughts without considering their effect on Mary. We brothers spoke our minds freely, unconcerned about each other's feelings.

Sometimes tempers flared. We knew we loved each other, but in business we didn't tiptoe around. Suddenly, I had to consider Mary's feelings and ideas before making decisions and check with her when making plans or schedules. A wife could get her feelings hurt a lot easier than a bunch of guys.

Journal, age 20

Boy, you've got to be careful with women.

Holding up my end of the bargain was easy compared to Mary's. Joining up with me, she was dumped right into the fish bowl with the rest of us. Perhaps the most dramatic part of public life during this time were the death threats we regularly received. Along with the news that Mary was to be my bride came threats on her life as well.

Journal, age 20

Mary is very nervous to say the least. A police car has been assigned to follow her around.

Shortly after our marriage, the Symbionese Liberation Army, a radical fringe group dedicated to freeing the planet of oppression, kidnapped publishing baron William Randolf Hearst's 19-year-old granddaughter. Demanding millions of dollars worth of food for the poor in exchange for her release, the SLA incident drew national media attention for months. But we never imagined our own family would be directly affected by it.

78

Journal, age 20

We have just been alerted by the FBI that we've received a major death threat from the SLA in regards to Patty Hearst's abduction. The whole family gathered to hear our options. They have demanded that certain Osmonds leave the entertainment business by a certain date or we will be killed. Patty is a fan I guess, and they got her diaries and are trying to destroy her thoughts and brainwash her. Well, what an interesting situation to have to deal with.

My brothers and I have been deputized and I just went to a shooting range to get certified to carry a weapon.

Journal, age 21

I have my pistol loaded and in ready position. It sure is sad to have to deal with crazy people.

Surprisingly, another problem was finances. At the time Mary and I were married, the Osmonds were worth many millions. But the bulk of it went into a central family fund used for investment purposes. Mary and I were given a small monthly allowance, just enough to survive on.

Journal, age 20

I took my sweetie to dinner and spent all of our money. No, I take it back. We have a buck and a half left. And it's only the third of February. So we better tighten our belts.

As the other brothers began to marry, the money problem came to a head. Understandably, each brother's wife began to voice her desire for privacy and independence. It was obvious we needed to find a way to divide the money, support ourselves, and make our own financial decisions and investments. Everyone knew the system had to change, but it still took years.

Mary learned overnight she didn't just marry me, she married my whole family. While most families may get together for Sunday dinners, casual visits, or holidays, Mary soon found every day was a full-blown family reunion.

Our first Christmas together, Mary and I were assigned to buy all the gifts for the family. We shopped 'til we dropped, amassing a tower of thoughtfully chosen, beautifully wrapped presents for each member of the Osmond clan. Breathing a great sigh of relief and accomplishment, I settled in to enjoy a special holiday watching everyone open their gifts. Christmas morning came, and to my dismay, I found I had neglected to pick out a single gift for my sweet new wife!

Not only did Mary have to share me with my family, she also had to share her husband with the world. She was immediately swept up in the business, helping with the fan letters that poured in weekly by the thousands. As she stuffed and addressed envelopes to girls she knew would tack the photo of her husband on their bedroom walls wishing they could spend just a few minutes with him, Mary was often wishing the same thing.

Whenever my wife and I finally had the chance to go out together, whether to a restaurant, mall, or church meeting, Mary knew she'd end up waiting while I signed autographs. Not only that, she often spent entire days and nights alone, unsure when I'd return from a marathon recording session or business meeting. To make matters worse, she also knew that when I got home I'd be exhausted, hungry, and uncommunicative.

Journal, age 21

Mary is getting very bored lately. I don't know what I should do. I have responsibilities with the Brothers but I must think about my responsibilities to my wife. I sure hope she can roll with the punches, because there are going to be a lot of them.

Even in the best of situations, maintaining a marriage is challenging. That's why it's so important to make a wholehearted commitment at the outset. In the music business, we refer to signing a contract as getting it inked. In putting our name to a document specifying certain obligations and benefits, we feel assured that each party will carry out its end of the bargain to the best of its ability. It's the same in marriage. The fine print doesn't mention the degree of difficulty, only that you're obliged to do your best.

There have been many times when it became imperative that I put aside personal convenience and individual goals in favor of a secure and healthy marriage relationship.

Journal, age 41

As I sit here tonight, so many thoughts are going through my mind. First, I want to say that I will give up everything to have the marriage I used to have. With the pressures weighing down on me like they have lately, the health concerns mounting and the cash flow problems, it's all taken its toll on me — and Mary. I believe this decision to move the family back to Utah and simplify my affairs will make my dreams come true. Nothing on this earth matters more to me than my relationship with my wife. This one issue has motivated this drastic change in career direction.

From the very beginning, Mary has endured more than her allotment of tests and trials due to my unusual lifestyle. Throughout our marriage, she has had to deal with my extensive traveling, financial ups and downs, and chronic health problems, at the same time doing the lion's share of raising our six children. It hasn't been easy. I believe it isn't meant to be. Mary and I have found marriage to be one of God's best refining methods.

What does my Heavenly Father mean to teach me through this sacred obligation? Nothing less than Christ's most basic doctrine of charity, or pure love. He who loves us perfectly asks us to love one another. And what more concentrated effort could there be than between husband and wife traveling together through this complex existence? For example, if I'm upset or dissatisfied with my wife, He asks me to look for the imperfection in myself, which could be of the subtlest nature. In wishing to transform her, I have the opportunity to find something that needs changing in myself, and to be motivated by God's love for me to work toward change.

I imagine this kind of talk is difficult to take if you are a victim of domestic abuse, but hear me out. God is counting on us to take care of ourselves. In allowing abuse of any kind, verbal, physical, emotional, spiritual, or financial, we may be enabling our spouse to treat us unkindly, to our own detriment and theirs. This distorted thinking can cause us to feel trapped and victimized. But by turning to Heavenly Father, we can learn how to change our thinking, and subsequently, our situation.

We can refuse to be controlled by someone else. Filled with confidence in God's love, we can take charge of our lives. There is help available through education from community, church, and law enforcement agencies. Much progress is being made in the area of domestic violence and abuse. The truth is, every human being has options, if only within the mind, that can create changes necessary to the peace and fulfillment God intends for us in this life.

There are indeed cases in which one partner or both are not willing to see marriage as the greatest opportunity for spiritual growth and enjoyment. By dishonoring the contract even in our very thoughts, the deal is compromised. Distractions that damage and destroy a marriage are everywhere: obsession with work, money, sports, entertainment, flirtations in the workplace, internet chat rooms, pornography, etc. All of these are symptoms of forgetting who we are and why we are here.

Whether one or both spouses fail dramatically, or just slip up day to day in little ways, marriage is there to test and try us, to draw us closer to God, to turn us to our Savior, and to seek spiritual guidance. Once we've inked our contract, it's up to us individually to honor and enjoy the life-changing results.

Journal, age 48

After 28 years of marriage I am more in love with my Mary than ever before. So many trials and strange situations have threatened to destroy our relationship. But with the Lord's help we have endured them all.

Hit Singles

CHILDREN

Marriage gave new depth to my wild lifestyle of recording, traveling, and performing. Suddenly, before me stretched a world of private hopes and dreams completely apart from my public image. More than anything, I wanted to be a father.

Mary and I were both raised in large families and planned to have a houseful of children of our own. We saw family as an important part of God's plan of happiness for us. Mary set about creating a comfortable home filled with love, learning, and faith. Like all newlyweds, we didn't anticipate the conflicts, problems, and heartaches that inevitably come with any family, at least to some degree. But we also didn't foresee the immeasurable joy God had in store.

From the moment our first child, Travis, was placed in my arms seconds after his birth, he consumed our lives. Everything we did revolved around this healthy little boy of ours and what we could do to make his life happy and complete.

Justin, our second child, had more trouble arriving. The delivery was premature and difficult. How grateful we were that he was safe — all five pounds of him. However, we soon began to notice in Justin a lack of response to certain sounds and loud noises. Concerned, we took him to the doctor only to learn our little son was 90 percent hearing-impaired. We were devastated.

I was no stranger to the idea of deafness, having grown up with two older brothers born with severe hearing problems. But this news affecting our own child sent both Mary and me into a tunnel of numbing grief that lasted for days. How could we handle this? Why did it happen? What did we do wrong?

Growing up I was vaguely aware of my parents' pioneering efforts in mainstreaming my brothers in a hearing world that would have had them institutionalized. I knew something of the many hours Mother had given teaching, encouraging, building confidence, and creating ways to help my brothers develop their own unique talents. The word "handicap" was not in my family's vocabulary. But knowing this weakness was genetic, I also remember thinking how difficult the whole situation was and hoping I'd never have a hearing-impaired child of my own.

Yet, here we were. In the midst of our sadness, we prayed to our loving Heavenly Father for meaning and direction. Comforting thoughts came to me from my childhood of fond memories of Virl and Tom, ages eight and six when I was born. I remembered following them around as fast as my legs could carry me. I'd watch them as they went about their chores. I dreamed of the day I'd be a big kid, too, able to do all the things they could do.

As I grew, Virl and Tom remained my idols. To me, they were geniuses who had earned their Duty to God and Eagle Scout awards. Why, they could do anything. For instance, the way they milked our cow was like a choreographed masterpiece. Sitting on stools on either side, Old Faye beat time by slapping their faces one after the other with her swishing tail. With four skilled hands poised on the udder, the milk hit the metal bucket with a rapid-fire rhythm that would put our tap dancing to shame.

A ray of insight broke through the gloom. I remembered with wonder that my brothers' lack of hearing hadn't slowed them down a bit. Suddenly Virl and Tom's struggles and victories, along with my parents' faith and ingenuity, began to benefit my own family in ways I had never dreamed. Strength, help, and meaning were within reach. I was given to know that Justin's challenges would prove to be a blessing to our family and to many others as well.

Still, as the years went by, I often wished I could take my son's burden upon myself. There were times when Justin's struggles brought me to my knees praying that his suffering would be alleviated. It has since occurred to me that this is precisely the reason for any of our troubles. They are an integral part of God's plan to turn us back to Him. He allows us to experience feelings and events, however dramatic, to get our attention and keep us on track.

Mary's educational background was a great blessing. With my extensive traveling, the task of not only raising our other children, but also giving special attention to Justin, fell mostly on her shoulders. She dove into the added challenge, working with him day and night, overcoming obstacles, traveling all over the country in search of the best technology and newest programs to help with his hearing needs.

Determined to mainstream Justin into a hearing world, just as my parents had done with Virl and Tom, we bypassed sign language and chose an auditory-verbal approach of communication with Justin. (He didn't learn any sign language at all until he was called at the age of nineteen to serve an LDS mission for the hearing-impaired in the United Kingdom.)

Armed with the latest research, Mary developed a pre-school called "A Child Shall Speak," for both hearing-impaired and normal-hearing kids. The children with normal hearing acted as models for those who were hearing-impaired, to show them that kids communicated through talking. During school, the hearing-impaired kids were pulled out of class for one-on-one time with a speech therapist.

Through years of tedious, often grueling speech therapy, Justin never complained. His bright, little-boy smile ever-present, he was eager to learn, always asking questions, improving one step at a time. I thanked my Heavenly Father for Mary's diligence and creativity and Justin's cheerful attitude as I witnessed the miracle of my son grasping skills and learning to communicate verbally.

Justin wore "over the ear" aids from 18 months to age 22. Along with these, he wore a rather cumbersome device during elementary school. It was a telecoil box that hung around his neck attached to his hearing aids. His teachers also wore a telecoil around their necks. Every word they spoke went directly to his hearing aids, even when he was out of the room. It wasn't until after he finished growing that Justin was able to be fitted with aids placed directly inside the ear canals.

We enrolled Justin in school and music lessons along with our other children as if he had no handicap. Beginning with the piano and violin, he eventually settled on the viola as he was better able to hear the lower tones. He performed in musical programs with his siblings all through his youth. During high school he played on the basketball and soccer teams, and was kicker on the football team. He also participated nationally in competitive soccer from age ten, won math awards, and earned his Eagle Scout Award.

Nothing has stopped Justin. He is a total people person, interacting easily with anyone and everyone. One Sunday afternoon, Justin stood at the pulpit speaking in a church meeting. A teary-eyed congregation heard from his own mouth how this boy's hearing impairment helped make him a better person. They heard him express faith in his Savior and his conviction that someday, when he meets him, he will be able to hear perfectly. "Won't that be great?" he said.

After graduating from Utah State University, Justin landed a job working as director of public relations for

Starkey Communications, a company which makes and sells hearing aids. He helps organize humanitarian efforts to the hearing-impaired in underdeveloped countries. On a trip to Peru recently, he wrote to us of an experience fitting the native children with hearing aids:

> . . . *we were scheduled to fit about 225 kids but ended up fitting 450, which is about 900 hearing aids. Boy, did it keep us busy. I took charge of the training and counseling, teaching the kids how to use the new hearing aids. I also took part in using the otoscope to check their ears to make sure they were clean before we made molds for them. I loved to see the kids faces light up as they could hear for the first time. It was truly a heart throbber.*
>
> *I remember talking with one family. The parents expressed full-heartedly how thankful they were for their 7-year-old daughter to have hearing. They were excited for her to reach her potential, to get a good education, to have opportunities to grow. The mother then said she wished to send her back to the states with me! I was blown away! She was willing to give her daughter up so she could have all the advantages available in America! I ended up telling her that she could do just what my mother had done for me, that is, teaching me every day, bit by bit, how to use my voice, how to form words, how to speak.*
>
> *— Email from Justin Osmond, November 2001*

Our son Justin, whom we so worried over, who struggled as a little boy to learn to use his voice and form words, now communicates with ease. He enthusiastically works to spearhead an effort which supplies twenty thousand hearing aids annually to children and adults who would otherwise spend their lives unfulfilled in a silent, lonely world. If we turn to Him, in time, Heavenly Father will open the way.

Much as we hoped for a large family, Mary's health became a problem during her third pregnancy and the arrival of Shane. We couldn't bear to think of not having any more children. Covering all the bases, we put off the surgery the doctor suggested for Mary, which would prevent our having more children of our own, and also put our names on adoption lists. We were delighted to be able to have two more babies. Heather arrived safely, a surprise daughter, rare for Osmonds, and then another son, Troy, after which surgery for Mary became unavoidable. Troy was a toddler when a friend called telling us about a baby girl. We gratefully welcomed Sheila, just days old, into our hearts and home, completing our family circle.

Why children? Why bring them into a world filled with trouble and suffering? Mary and I believe children are another part of that great plan I've been talking so much about. In a pre-earth existence, every one of us, as spirits, chose mortality so we could experience a world of opposition. For every good there is evil; for every pain there is joy. We could not know one without the other.

In His divine omniscience, God exposes us to this opposition to fulfill His grand design, that of His children's growth and progression. In the eternal sense, the children we care for with such emotion and energy are not our own. We think they belong to us, but they are God's. They are only entrusted to us for a time as an ennobling and demanding assignment to nurture, teach, and serve them out of love for Him.

Truly, parenthood is part of our earthly test, each child a unique individual. While we can teach and be examples to our children, we cannot control many of the circumstances surrounding them or force our children to behave as we wish they would. We can use our experiences as parents to draw closer to or further away from God, to become more or less like Christ.

Journal, age 40

I lost my temper big time with Travis. Dark clouds, tornado winds, and lighting rolled in while he and the other boys were out on the boat. It wasn't until the last second before calling the police that they showed up. Boy, did I let Travis have it. I told him I couldn't trust him. He's only eighteen, in charge of a group of kids on a lake in a boat with a tornado beating down. What was I supposed to say? When he could get a word in, he told me the engines had died and they had to wait for someone to tow them in to shore. He's sick about the whole thing and so am I. Lightning just hit the hotel

*next to us, and shut off the power. I feel darkness in
more ways than one.*

*Later. I visited with Travis. I just leveled with him
and told him that I really overreacted and that I love him
so much. I know why Travis was sent to us first. He's
my leader. Everything worked out.*

Thank goodness children are resilient. More importantly, thank goodness we as earthly stewards of God's
children have a loving, all-encompassing Savior. Because of
Jesus Christ, we can turn to our Father in Heaven in our
errors, receive forgiveness, and feel an outpouring of love.

By focusing on the truth that our children belong to
God and we are His helpers regarding them, we can avoid
the trap of becoming defined by our children's circumstances, successes, or failures. Though we will surely experience pleasure in their accomplishments, frustration in
their failings, and sorrow in their struggles, these things
must never cross over into our feelings of personal worth. If
our value is centered on our kids, we'll surely be tossed to
and fro with every hint of a storm. All that is required to
stay steady is to remember who we are, that our worth is
not measured by the results of our parenting, and that all
these experiences are for our refinement.

God in His perfect patience allows us as parents time to
grieve losses. Although he gives us opportunities to fumble
through emotions and errors, we can press forward in the

midst of our deep feelings with hope in an ultimate joyous outcome, and with plenty of enjoyment along the way.

Here are some recent emails from my kids. I don't think it gets any better than this:

Maggon (daughter-in-law): Happy Birthday, Father! Sorry Trav and I woke you up so early. We wanted to sing you happy birthday before he left for work. I love you, Father! And I thank my Heavenly Father every day that my husband was taught so well. In my opinion, you and Mother created a masterpiece in your family, the oldest son especially.

Me: Justin, Have I told you lately how much I love you? *Justin (24): Yes, Father! I will always know that! If anything ever happens, the bond that holds us together will last forever.*

Shane and Brittney (newlyweds): Father, Britt and I just wanted to tell you how blessed we are to have you in our lives. Just a call from you brightens up our days. Thank you so much for teaching me how to be a gentleman. We want to model our marriage after yours. You are the best father in the world.

Heather (19): My Dear Daddy, I am sitting here thinking about you as you are in surgery right now. I just want you to know how much you mean to me. I love you more than words can express. Last night when we were just laughing on your bed was one of the best times of my life. We don't need everything. We just need each other's love.

Troy (17): *Dear Father, Have I told you that I loved you today?*

Sheila (14): *Dear Father, Thank you so much for getting after me. I don't know what I would do without you.*

Email from me to my kids, 2001: *Dear family, I love the way you all keep in touch with each other. Please stay close. Don't let anything come between you. Talk things out before they fester. Forgive and forget the many stupid things we sometimes say to each other. They don't mean a thing in the big picture. Goodnight my wonderful children.*

𝓕𝒶𝓃 𝓒𝓁𝓊𝒷

FRIENDS

Journal, age 22

It's a first! A freight company delivered a huge box.
There were people inside! Fans mailed themselves to us!

It would be nice if everybody had a fan club, or something like it. Perhaps you have a circle of old friends or a
support group of new acquaintances, a cluster of colleagues
or a crowd of co-workers, a throng of family or a single con-
fidant. Maybe you've seen friends come and go or experienced a falling out with family members. Maybe you'd like
to improve family relationships or acquire more friends.

Since 1992, my brothers and I have performed in
Branson, Missouri. Dancers and singers work behind us as
we entertain from the front of the stage. During some of our
numbers, we move into the audience to shake hands with as
many wonderful fans as we can. It is not unusual to be
greeted with great enthusiasm, members of the audience
yelling and screaming in the excitement of the moment. Of
course we always thank them and move along.

During one such performance, when we had an ice rink behind us, I ventured out as usual into the audience deciding to take on the first row. Shaking hands with one nice lady, I particularly noticed her screaming. Wishing to show my appreciation I leaned toward her, saying, "Oh, thank you, thank you!" But she wailed even louder. Tears came running down her face. Just then, I looked down and saw that I was stepping on her shoe. The ice picks on the bottom of my shoe were digging into her foot! Despite good intentions, I was actually hurting her.

One day I sat down with an individual I had known for years. I thought our friendship was strong until he started in on me. Why had it been so long since he had heard from me, he wanted to know. Why didn't I call anymore? "I thought you were my friend," he said.

At first I was thrown for a loop. Cancelling my next appointment to spend more time with him, I found myself apologizing all over the place, but no amount of apologizing seemed to satisfy him. Frustrated, my thoughts turned to Jesus Christ, a man of sorrows, rejected by his friends. Somehow we got into a discussion about how Jesus loved everyone regardless of how they treated him. Our conversation ended with an agreement to re-establish our friendship based on that unconditional love Christ exemplified.

Elvis Presley once told my brothers and me that if he could do it all over again, he would sign every autograph and shake every hand that was extended to him. It's a nice sentiment, but sad to say, it can't be done. We simply can't be all things to all people. Whether it's time, energy, money, or awareness, we don't have the resources to take care of everyone's needs and desires.

With every human relationship, there comes the risk of unfulfilled expectations. Since we are imperfect, try as we might, it is inevitable that we will fail one another in some way at some time, especially if our expectations are too high. To avoid falling into Elvis's dilemma, we can use God's love to rid ourselves of excessive dependencies on others and learn to detach from others' inordinate dependencies on us. The truth is we are not responsible for what others may perceive about us if we are doing our best. Our job is to cultivate kind feelings toward others no matter what.

I have a dear friend, Dale Gunderson. We hardly ever get together, but when we do it's as if we've never been apart. Good feelings abound as we catch up on each other's lives. There are no expectations, just genuine fondness and concern. It's great.

In another instance, a wonderful, dynamic friend of mine all at once lost the confidence of many who depended on him. Filled with concern for the well-being of my friend, I prayed for direction. My answer was to refrain from judging, that I didn't have sufficient knowledge to understand all that had happened. I was given the impression that this great man's trials were his own to endure. My job was to feel at peace with my long-time friend, and show him loving kindness amid the persecution he was experiencing.

How much more enjoyable our relationships would be if we let go of expectations and practiced unqualified kindness. If we have a strained relationship, it's a good bet we can find something in ourselves that requires tweaking. I'm convinced that whenever I'm upset or complaining about someone else's faults or failings, it's me who has the most urgent problem. This doesn't mean that others don't have big problems that need correction, but the point is, they aren't complaining. If my inner peace is compromised, I have work to do within my heart. I am not tuned in to God's love. I need to exercise faith by turning to the Lord for guidance and direction.

With reduced expectations and God's love for all people filling our hearts, I have an idea that everyone's personal fan club would grow by leaps and bounds, though they may not come by Federal Express.

Homesick

GUIDANCE

Journal, age 33

I just had to leave Mary and the kids again for a four-week tour. To see the tears run down my wife's face and my kids holding on to my legs tore my heart into pieces. It looks like I'll be gone nine months out of this year. What a strange business I'm in.

This was just one of many tearful partings my family and I have endured. Due to the nature of the entertainment business, I've spent much of my life traveling. When I'm home I get to be with my family around the clock, but on the road I may go for weeks, or even months, without seeing them. Being away from my wife and children for any length of time has always been difficult.

In the early '80s, the four original Osmond brothers toured around the country. Later in the decade, I produced and performed on my own, including a TV special. Then, in 1992, Jimmy suggested that we brothers get back together and perform six days a week at his theater in Branson, Missouri. We were instantly attracted to Branson because of its emphasis on family entertainment. With the decision to take Jimmy's offer, we moved our families from Utah to Branson where we lived for about five years.

Though we enjoyed living permanently in Branson, several factors seemed to necessitate moving my family back to Utah while I continued commuting to perform. It had been so wonderful being together day-to-day that Mary and I struggled with the decision. In addition to personal and family prayer, I sought advice and priesthood blessings from my Bishop and other church leaders for guidance. Still, I struggled.

One day I woke up with the thought of calling Gordon B. Hinckley for some advice. Though I was personally acquainted with President Hinckley, the spiritual leader of our Church, I knew he was a very busy man. My idea to call him was about the equivalent of a member of the Catholic Church calling the Pope with some personal problem. I brushed it off as a dumb idea.

Later, on my knees by my bed, I felt that prompting again to call President Hinckley. I picked up the phone and dialed the Church Office Building, my heart beating fast. I told the secretary who I was, hoping she would take a message, but soon President Hinckley was on the line.

"Well, hello, Merrill," he said.

"Oh, President, I am so grateful you would take a minute of your time," I said feeling sheepish.

He listened patiently as I described my dilemma. After a while the other end of the phone quieted.

"Brother Osmond," he said, "I think I have a thought for you."

"Oh, wonderful! I'll follow any advice you can give me."

"Brother Osmond," he said again, "I can't help you. You know how to get an answer from the Lord. Go to your knees, ask Him, and He will direct you."

Here I was, hoping for a rescuer, someone to take away my burden, fix all my problems, and what does he do but turn my life right back over to me! President Hinckley, knowing he had the power to guide my life, respected my agency above all, and I was grateful for the reminder of God's plan.

We're given problems as a means of turning to our Heavenly Father. I was wishing He would send me a black-and-white solution such as to leave the entertainment business and try something new to earn a living. But solutions to mortal dilemmas do not usually come in neatly wrapped and quickly delivered packages. Sometimes we have to plug along in our given circumstances, exercising faith that there is something to be learned. Other times, an answer is forthcoming that we don't want to hear. We may learn much later, after the trial of our faith, what the purpose was behind our trouble.

Journal, age 34

I just checked into my hotel room. I have become familiar with a hotel room over the years. I often wonder why my life has to be so. My children asked me why I have to be gone so much. I've wept many tears and spent many lonely hours on my knees to know the answer. Why couldn't I have been a farmer?

Gradually, over months, the answer to my prayer settled in my mind like a first snow covers the earth with a layer of white. I didn't even see it coming, but suddenly I knew. God would have me commute to Missouri while my family returned and settled in our Utah home. He let me know my children were grounded and thriving, well taken care of by my marvelous, faithful, long-suffering wife. Yes, it was inconvenient, it was heart wrenching, and it was less than ideal, but it was all right.

Nothing had changed except my perception. I felt God knew me and knew my trials; I knew that my Savior would strengthen me as I waded through them, leaning on him along the way. It was lonely and difficult at times, but it was the life Heavenly Father had planned for me. That conviction made it all worthwhile.

Journal, age 44

My life has become much more relaxed since I decided to let go and trust in the Lord. Living back in Utah in this tiny town has helped too. I just love being here with my family, even though I can't be here all the time. There are days when I can't get our car out of the driveway because a herd of sheep is making its way

toward the hills. Other times the neighbors assemble on
our corner just to talk. I love lying on the trampoline in
the back yard and gazing at the night sky filled with a
galaxy of stars.

I like to think of this life as a business trip away from
home, one in which we are called to perform our own
particular duties on an earthly stage. I'm reminded of our
opening night in Branson, Missouri. We hadn't performed
together for a while and I was a little nervous.

Journal, age 39

When the reality hit that the show was about to
start, an amazing amount of stress hit me hard. Sure I
have a lifetime of experience in show production, but I
was on edge the whole day. Was everything ready? Did
I do all I could? Were my brothers prepared? Were the
back up plans in place in case we needed to adjust while
on stage? Were the technical people on top of every
little detail? Minutes before the show I was hit with a
barrage of questions. Concerned people ran up to me
inquiring about things only I could respond to.

It had been so long since we performed together.
There in the audience sat the press, our competitors
from other theaters, the local residents that either make
or break you in this town. My energy levels were climb-
ing. But looking into the faces of my brothers, we
exchanged a simple smile that set me at ease. Yes, there

were problems and mistakes, but the overall objective was accomplished.

Only when we forget that this performance is only temporary, and that we are humanly incapable of perfection, do we get stage fright. I've spoken to many people afflicted with such cases of nervousness: a man who wanted to take his life because he lost his fortune in a business transaction, a young woman whose husband left her, a friend who was unfaithful to his wife, a mother of young children serving a criminal sentence in prison. Problems like these can easily make us panic; we feel our lives are beyond our control.

When we remember who we are and how much we are loved and accepted regardless of our performance, the uneasiness disappears. We know these hot, bright lights are not all there is. Individual guidance is available from above to give meaning to our efforts while we remain here on earth, however homesick we may be for our heavenly home.

Journal, age 29

We have been riding on this bus for two days straight. I have no idea where we're going and I'm getting carsick. I have this bunk that's sitting over the engine and fumes come right through the vent next to me. I miss my family at home so much. I have a picture taped to the ceiling over my head to remind me of their little faces. If I didn't know the importance of what I'm doing, you couldn't pay me enough to do it.

Plugged In

FAITH

Journal, age 26

We had a terrible scare tonight. Father was the target for a hit. Coming home from rehearsal, Mary and I were strolling along an outdoor walkway that led to our hotel rooms. There on the third floor we saw Father standing in a window opening rocking our little Travis and holding him to his chest. I was the one who saw it first. There in the trees just below was a man dressed in a black outfit, wearing black gloves and a ski hat, holding a rifle pointed at Father. I screamed out, "Hit the deck!" The man with the gun very calmly turned toward the sound of my voice, lowered the gun, uncocked it, and walked out of the courtyard. By the time the police arrived he had slipped away.

Sometimes life can get so scary that we want to hit the deck or, in other words, give up or even turn away from God in anger and grief. Our faith may waver as we worry about what incomprehensible danger, pain, or loss is waiting in the shadows like some random sniper dressed in black. Harsh as it may sound, this is part of the plan. We're here as mortal beings to experience a variety of things we cannot control, including consequences that result from others' choices.

We have our agency to choose how we will react to what we see as unexplainable events. It's up to us to exercise faith in a God who knows us, loves us, and has only our long-term well-being in mind. Human as we are, without the benefit of God's omniscience, many times we don't understand why things happen the way they do. But if we stay plugged in to His strengthening, comforting spirit, we'll know in time.

I've enjoyed producing many types of entertainment, from youth pageants on football fields to TV Specials. It can get pretty complicated when you're working with tech crews, performers, costumes, props, lights, videos, scripts, cues, etc. I've found that whether we're producing a show, working in an office, driving a truck, doing the dishes, caring for others, struggling with grief, or writing a book, the same principles apply. All things belong to God; we can be consciously serving Him in everything we do. Here's one such experience I had in learning to connect with the will of God and stay on task despite the proverbial sniper, or a whole army of them.

In 1980, when Governor Reagan came to Salt Lake City wrapping up his campaign for the Presidency of the United

States, my family received a call from the Reagan committee asking the Osmonds to meet with him. Gathering together from all over the state for this meeting, we were ushered into a room where Governor Reagan was waiting. He told us of his desire that we participate in his inaugural activities, should he be elected. He hoped we would perform and perhaps produce some of the events that would surround the momentous occasion. After this meeting, I wrote in my journal, *I am taking this very seriously.* I was 27.

When Reagan won the election our whole family was pleased and excited. I called the Inaugural Committee to ask what events were scheduled and where the Osmonds could get involved. Perhaps because of confusion surrounding the change of command at the White House, no one seemed very helpful. Nevertheless, we were invited to Washington D.C. to meet with the committee.

My assistant Bill Critchfield, Mary, and I walked into a large room filled with inaugural committee members. Asked what we wanted to do for the President, I responded that he had expressed a wish that we get involved in producing some of the events. With that, one individual said, "We don't need anyone's help right now. We have all the producers we need." They then thanked us for our efforts in the campaign and dismissed us.

At this point, I was advised to step back. People told me that I would never be able to penetrate the bureaucracy surrounding the inaugural events, and that I should just go home and forget the whole thing. Most of the family agreed, but something inside me rejected this idea. I was not about to let this opportunity go without a fight. I knew President Reagan wanted us to help, and I felt God wanted us involved too.

I arranged another meeting with the committee, and presented a few ideas that had never before been done at an inaugural, such as an opening ceremony. Hearing this idea, the committee agreed it was good, but assured me there were no extra finances available to make it happen. I finally persuaded the group to give me a little time to raise the money. I didn't know until I got back home to Utah that I only had one month to raise two and a half million dollars.

Planting myself on the couch with the phone growing out of my ear, I attempted to contact everyone I could think of who might have an interest in this event and would wish to contribute any amount. Many times I fell asleep waiting on hold, but the money was not materializing.

In addition to fundraising, I set about planning the event. I envisioned a parade, entertainment, fireworks, and, what else? The Mormon Tabernacle Choir. I called church headquarters and talked to Gordon B. Hinckley, who was then a counselor to President Kimball, to get his input on the idea. He informed me that the choir would be on tour in Japan at that time, but he promised to discuss it with his council and get back to me. I heard back from him shortly with the news that they would like to see the choir perform at the Inaugural if the proper funding was available. Despite my discouragement over the money problem,

I had a strong feeling things would come together somehow.

A few days later, I received another phone call from Gordon B. Hinckley reporting that a letter had arrived from the Inaugural Committee uninviting the choir. "What is this all about?" he wanted to know, having already made arrangements to change the choir's schedule. Perplexed and embarrassed, I did my best to reassure him.

"Don't worry. I'll get this resolved," I said, wondering why the committee seemed bent on ignoring President Reagan's wishes. What was going on?

Determined to clear up this mess with the Tabernacle Choir, I was up the next morning at 6:00 phoning the White House. After ten calls to the main switchboard, and a series of transfers from office to office, a good friend, Dick Andrews, finally put me through to Nancy Reagan's assistant. I pleaded my case with her, hoping she could intercede.

Journal, age 27

I received a call from Gordon B. Hinckley this morning. He got another letter from the Inaugural Committee re-inviting the choir! I think I've lost ten pounds these last few days, but my faith is increasing. I'm going forward with it!

Feeling encouraged, I renewed my fundraising efforts. With the choir's appearance scheduled, I went to visit prominent Church member Willard Marriott. Explaining how I was producing the opening inaugural events and that the Tabernacle Choir had been invited by Ronald Reagan to perform, I boldly asked him to contribute fifty thousand dollars to the cause.

Hearing about the choir, he became visibly upset and began relating a similar story of his involvement in the Nixon Inaugural. The January weather had turned on him; hailstorms and high winds had ruined the proceedings, and he felt he had embarrassed the Church. Not only would he withhold his support, he told me he would try to stop me from trying. Well, all I could do was apologize for the intrusion and leave. Such disparaging remarks from someone I respected and admired devastated me. Still, I felt God's Spirit urging me to keep trying.

Determined to make much needed headway, I again camped out in the family room with the telephone, night and day. I called people all over the United States while Mary served my meals where I sat in my pajamas, glued to the couch. With dismay, I found that those who had resources made excuses to bow out, while those with very little gave freely. This wasn't getting me far at all. I remember feeling totally beaten, my body bent over in exhaustion, my head laid wearily on the coffee table, when the phone rang. It was a man named Karl Lindner, president of a major insurance company.

"Is this Merrill Osmond?" he asked.

"Yes, sir," I answered, suddenly revived.

"Are you the one putting the Inaugural Opening Ceremony together?"

"Yes, sir," I said again.

"How much do you need?" I heard him say, my mouth dropping open.

With a gasp I responded, "Mr. Lindner! As much as I can get!"

Our conversation turned to the Inaugural itself along with his interest in televising the events. Then came the words that floored me.

"How about $700,000?"

In an instant my fundraising days were all but wrapped up. Built on this generous donation, the rest of the money practically raised itself.

The week of President Reagan's inauguration arrived. The opening event I had planned was to feature the Tabernacle Choir accompanied by the United States Army Band, singing *America the Beautiful*, *Battle Hymn of the Republic*, and *The Star Spangled Banner*. All this would occur on the marble steps of the shining white Lincoln Memorial to a choreographed firework and cannon show set against a flag-blue, starry night sky. Or so I hoped.

Though I had overcome all the obstacles placed in my path so far, Brother Marriot's argument suddenly loomed larger than Lincoln himself. Ice storms raged, winds howled, and crowds began leaving the area bitten by below freezing temperatures. Just as things couldn't get any worse, a section of scaffolding collapsed to the ground, tragically killing a bystander. The Secret Service moved in and cancelled the entire event. I began to think I had committed an enormous blunder.

Taking my wife Mary by the hand, I led her into a trailer and together we knelt to pray. As we were pouring our hearts out to our Father in Heaven, we heard pounding on the door.

"Osmond? Are you in there? The President is on his way and we can't stop him. Clean everything up. We're back on!"

I grabbed a walkie-talkie and directed instructions to the sound and firework crews. Just as we finished plugging everything back in, here came the President and his entourage. As the music began, a miracle occurred. The clouds parted and the winds died. My father, who stood next to me, looked from the clear sky to my face with tears in his eyes. That was it for me. I wept right along with him.

While my family and I performed the next night along with other entertainers at a gala celebration, my mind wandered to the events yet to come that I had worked so hard to organize. Our studio in Utah had combined with a construction company in the east to design the largest parade float ever built. My team and I were in charge of getting the 300-voice Tabernacle Choir on the enormous 110-foot float to provide the grand finale to the 100-piece Inaugural parade. At the President's request, the choir was to stop before the big glassed-in review stand where he was sitting, and sing the *Battle Hymn of the Republic*.

Things seemed to go smoothly as the float sailed along Pennsylvania Avenue to the delight of an enthusiastic crowd. Spectators along the parade route called out for the choir to "Sing, sing!" and were treated time and again to grand, goose-bump-raising refrains. Suddenly, my right-hand man came running up to me totally out of breath.

"Merrill, Merrill," he gasped. "The Inaugural Committee found out we had permission to stop the float in front of the President, and they went ballistic! They put the order out that under no circumstance will the float stop. What are we going to do?"

A thought popped into my head. I asked him how much money he had on him. He reached into his pocket and pulled out a fifty-dollar bill. I found I had a fifty also.

"Look," I said, "you have a red badge. The Secret Service will allow you to get close to the float. You've got to get to the tractor driver and hand him this fifty bucks. Tell him if he floods the tractor on the 'X' you'll give him another fifty." My dear friend stared at me dumbfounded.

"Go, go!" I said. He went.

Just as the float moved within a few feet of the President's stand I heard the tractor's engine begin to sputter and stall. As planned, the *Battle Hymn of the Republic* rang out through the wintry afternoon directly in front of the hours-old President of the United States. National television caught him blinking back the tears and wiping his eyes with his hand. It was estimated that ninety million people witnessed the Tabernacle Choir sing at the Inaugural. My methods may have been a little unconventional, but I felt the Lord's truth had truly marched on.

That night the President invited our family to the White House for a celebration party. When Mary and I saw President Reagan motion for me to come over, I walked right into a circle where several of the Inaugural Committee stood. I wasn't at all surprised when they all seemed to avoid eye contact with me. The President graciously expressed his appreciation for the opening events, especially for bringing the choir back to sing his favorite song, saying it was the highlight of the Inaugural.

Full of gratitude to my Heavenly Father, I felt impressed to say, "President, without the support of these fine gentlemen here, it never would have happened." With that, President Reagan turned to the group and thanked them for making the event so special. I never heard from them again.

Back home in Utah, I received a call from Gordon B. Hinckley. Though he was pleased with the choir's contribution to the Inaugural, he told me that $50,000 of the needed funds had never materialized as promised. Mortified, I told him I'd get right on it. Chuckling, he added, "Never mind, Merrill. Brother Marriott came through."

Technical Problems

EXPERIENCE

Journal, age 31

Independence, Missouri. A strange thing happened at our outdoor concert. With 10,000 people sitting on the grass watching our show, a storm came up. Behind our stage sat a rack of firework shells aimed at the sky for a patriotic finale. No one noticed the wind blow the rack down. Now the shells were aimed not only at our backs but at the entire audience. On cue, the shells left their casings and started blowing up through the middle of our band. Fireworks exploded ten feet above people's heads. Everyone was screaming. After ten minutes of what seemed like nuclear war, the explosions stopped and the strangest thing happened. The crowd started roaring. They thought it was part of the show! Our drummer had a direct hit to his rear end and ended up in the hospital.

As a child, I was trained to entertain large crowds. Out of necessity, I developed a certain confidence and trust in people that they'd appreciate and respond to what we had worked so hard to prepare. The applause clinched it. It meant they sincerely liked what we did. I came to rely on that straightforward form of communication. This blind trust extended off stage. When someone smiled and looked me in the eye, I believed what they said. However, dealing with people in real life is much more complicated, subject to technical problems, you might say.

After the first highly successful season of *The Donny and Marie Show* back in 1976–77, which we produced in Los Angeles, we decided to move back to Utah. There we could be surrounded by the values and standards we cherished, build our own television studio and produce the show, as well as expand our creativity to other projects.

Several people tried to discourage us. Where would we find the talent in Utah, they argued. It was a huge undertaking, but we were filled with confidence. We had many years of experience producing shows, connections with key people, and the financial resources we needed to make it happen. Unfortunately, we were also naive.

After five years in operation, the Osmond Studio that had been such a dream come true turned into a financial nightmare. While we Osmonds were busy creating and producing, our financial matters had gotten out of hand. Millions of dollars seemed to disappear into thin air. People we had trusted over the years and business associates we had leaned on lost their credibility, bringing us down with them. We were unaware of the ulterior motives, risky investments, and poor decisions of our associates, which finally took their toll.

I felt the burden of responsibility and found myself in the middle of it all, trying to salvage whatever I could to keep everyone afloat. As a result, though we were grateful to avoid bankruptcy, we ended up with nothing.

Journal, age 29

These are sad days. The Osmond Studio is ready to close. There is so much debt on the building it would take a miracle to find the cash flow to service it. When everyone was gone, I walked through the building and wept. So many hard lessons have been learned these days. When you lose everything, you change inside. I'm proud of my family. Good things can come from our losses. I just know it.

During this difficult time, one day was especially trying. I hadn't been feeling well. My response to the mounting financial pressures had resulted in bleeding ulcers and high blood pressure. I returned home from the studio, problems racing around in my mind. Losing my temper over a petty disagreement with Mary, I retreated to our room and sat alone on our bed. Suddenly I went completely numb, my body heavy as lead. I felt myself lying there staring at the ceiling, but I couldn't move a muscle. My eyes felt propped open with toothpicks, unable to blink. Try as I might, I couldn't seem to get enough air into my lungs.

I could see Mary in the room, but she appeared far away. She seemed to be slapping me in the face, although I couldn't feel it. She asked me questions in a strange slow voice, an octave lower than normal, her face distorted. I tried to answer her but couldn't move my lips to form the words. Sweat poured from my scalp, colors flashed and faded. It seemed my only task was to lie there gasping for breath, allowing my heart to take over my body as it beat like a giant bass drum, louder and faster, so loud and fast I was sure it would explode.

I was aware of people running into the bedroom, an oxygen mask on my face, a needle in my arm, being strapped onto a table and wheeled out of the house into an ambulance. My unblinking eyes filled, overflowed, and emptied—a sort of involuntary weeping. I began to pray to my Heavenly Father that I might be spared this awful situation. I wondered if it was my time to go. Random scenes from my life and family played like a choppy home video through my mind.

Once in the hospital, I was treated with various shots and given a series of tests. Doctors found a blood vessel had closed off in my neck causing a mini-stroke. Inserting a needle into my chest, they also drained a build-up of fluid around my heart which they concluded was caused by emotional stress. Under sedation, I drifted off into my first real sleep in many days.

I was released the next morning under doctor's orders to avoid any pressure or strain. This was easier said than done. Talking Mary into letting me go, I caught a plane to Arizona the next day to do a previously scheduled show with my brothers and Marie. I was feeling fine, with only a slight tenderness from the needle in my chest.

The short flight gave me some time to think. The frightening loss of control over my faculties felt like a warning. What was Heavenly Father trying to teach me? Our financial collapse aside, could I have done something to prevent or ease the build-up of mental and emotional stress on my mind and body?

The answer is yes. Though we may have to accept and submit to circumstances, we need not become emotional and spiritual casualties because of them. It isn't so much what happens to us that matters to our basic well-being. What matters more is how we perceive what happens to us, or what we tell ourselves about the events. Although it is necessary to our health and growth that we face our troubles and allow whatever time we need to work our way through periods of unblinking shock and grief, it is ultimately helpful to keep spiritual truths foremost in our minds.

Any trouble we deny will come back to haunt us in one way or another. By stressing out, giving up, escaping, or growing bitter, we may avoid some present pain, but also lose great opportunities to grow and to feel peace and joy. Because of a few technical problems, we may miss the best parts of the show.

It was 4:30 P.M., after we had performed a matinee show in Branson, when I received a phone call from a dear friend.

She was crying so hard on the other end of the line I couldn't understand what she was saying. Able to extract from her an address, which was about a mile away from the theater, I told her I would be right there. Her warning, "No! Don't come! It's over!" made up my mind. Once at the hotel, I ran to her room and banged on the door. There was no answer, not even a sound. I continued knocking. Finally, to my surprise the door slowly began to open, framing a shocking sight. My friend, white-faced, held a gun to her head.

In a quiet voice I told her to give me the gun. She refused. I continued speaking to her, moving into the room inch by inch. Engaging her in a conversation, I found she was confused, her mind filled with lies and discouragement. It was forty-five minutes later that she finally put down the weapon.

Though we may have weaknesses that may stimulate crises like this one, there is help available. Sometimes we need professional help. In this woman's case, she called a friend. We always have options. Giving up doesn't have to be one of them.

Besides help from others, which may not be constant or reliable, we have an even better source to turn to for support. God, our Father in Heaven, loves us. Our Lord and Savior knows our suffering. There is nothing They don't understand regarding our troubles and trials.

We agreed to experience this opposition here on earth to prove that our love for God would exceed any loss or disappointment, contradiction or pain. We are asked to suspend our own logic and expectations and instead put our trust in a higher intelligence. We can let go intellectually, hang on spiritually, and put heart over mind.

The rewards for submitting to trials out of love for God and faith in His plan are quiet, but they are sweet above all things. If we keep these truths foremost in our minds, there's a good chance we'll handle our problems more effectively, stay healthier, be available to help others and, most of all, feel an outpouring of God's love and His acceptance of our humble efforts.

Is there a way to prepare for these huge refining experiences so we can better handle them when they hit us head-on? Yes, by practicing on the mini-adversities. God gives them to us everyday. Getting a flat tire, burning the toast, forgetting an appointment, having the electricity shut off while watching the Super Bowl on TV, and a thousand other mishaps, missteps, and miscues. Believe it or not, they're all chances to turn to God, to remember His plan, to feel His love, and to go forward with faith. The miracle happens when we recognize the purpose of these events and change our reaction from annoyance and resentment to patience and understanding.

On the stage, things often go haywire. But when you're standing in front of a concert hall full of people, no matter what happens, you learn the meaning of the words, "the show must go on!" The entertainment business supplies plenty of opportunities to practice on the mini-adversities. Here are a few from my experience.

At one of our shows in Sweden, none of our backstage helpers spoke English. Though we had told them which side each brother would exit the stage during the show, when we came off for a change of sweaters, they had mixed them all up. Alan had to squeeze into Jimmy's, Donny had Alan's on, which hung to the floor. As if that wasn't frustrating enough, Alan came hurrying offstage with his saxophone just as I was running on. I caught the bell of that sax right in the head, causing a superficial but messy wound.

My least favorite venues were rodeos. The facilities are always iffy and tough to work around. At one particular gig we were told to move out into the arena right after the Brahma bull rides. The clowns took a break from distracting the bulls as they rolled us in a wagon toward the stage.

It happened to be raining, harder and harder every minute. Halfway to the stage, the wheels of our wagon got stuck in the mud. There we were, stranded, in our brand new white bell-bottomed costumes. We got out of the wagon and made our way to the stage as best we could, the crowd whooping and hollering at our predicament.

Finally on stage, we found we had no electricity. We had electric amps, guitars, and microphones, but no juice. The crowd went wild with laughter. Our drummer started playing some rhythms trying to get some clapping going when, all of a sudden, a huge Brahma bull got loose and headed for the stage. Did I mention we were wearing red jackets over our white pants? Our drummer picked up the beat. Riders appeared with ropes swinging. Clowns jumped onto the stage, yelling at us to hit the deck and lie still. The bull was lassoed just short of smashing the drummer.

Large or small, when things go wrong my first impulse is to ask God *why*. Why, when I've done my best, do things turn out differently than I planned? Though it's a difficult mental process requiring faith, prayer, and a humble change of heart, I've found it much more beneficial to submit to my circumstances. Instead of asking *why*, I ask *what*. Even if we're wearing red and a bull is galloping toward us, we can ask *What shall I do now, Father?*

From a spiritual perspective there are no bad experiences. Like the fireworks that went haywire, we can change our perception and find it's all part of the show.

Exposure

VALUES

Journal, age 16

We played an outdoor fair today and the sun was so hot, buckets of sweat came pouring off our heads. Father ordered us all soda to drink. I took my glass and chugged it down in one gulp. It tasted terrible! Later on we found out the waiter made a mistake. He gave us gin instead of pop! I'm in shock!

We enjoyed the peak of our performing and recording career during the 1970s, a decade on the heels of U.S. involvement in Vietnam when an anti-war, anti-establishment sentiment raged among young people. Rebellion demonstrated itself in the unrestrained use of drugs, sex, and alcohol, further fueled by popular music and the permissive lifestyle of many of its stars.

As active members of our church, we adhere to a health code we call the Word of Wisdom, which instructs us to abstain from substances harmful to the body. In addition, we promise to uphold high moral standards in all areas of our lives. As a result, we Osmonds stuck out in the '70s rock culture like a glass of milk in a bar. Perhaps more than our music, it was our church, our name, and our values that defined us wherever we went. Newspaper headlines all over the world emphasized our peculiarities. One such headline appearing in 1974 read, "Osmond Family Maintains Wholesome Image Despite Fame."

Journal, age 23

We performed in Munich, Germany last night. After the show we were invited to go to a restaurant and eat. Well, when we got to this place, we found out it was known for its 101 kinds of German beer. They took us in the back and asked us what kind of beer we wanted. When we said no, one of our hosts said, "C'mon, no one even knows you're here. Have some beer on us tonight. It is a part of our culture!" We finally convinced them that apple juice would do just fine. Today in the paper the headline said, "Osmonds Prefer Apple Juice to Munich Beer!"

The squeaky-clean Osmonds, with our big smiles and bubbly personalities, became the brunt of jokes on TV talk shows and sitcoms. I guess people thought we were too goody-goody to be true, and labeled us "square." As a result, we were often uninvited to celebrity parties. I guess some people decided that having us there would be uncomfortable.

None of this bothered us much. My father always said, "Put nine sticks together and try to break them all at once. It can't be done. Then take one stick and see how easy it breaks. Stick together." It wasn't difficult to stand up for our beliefs, especially with each other to rely on.

Another challenge we faced in the entertainment world was holding fast to our standards of decency. After *The Andy Williams Show,* when we were struggling to break into pop music, we sat in the offices of Warner Brothers Records and were presented with a song that was sure to be a hit no matter who recorded it. Listening to the music, we found some of the lyrics unsuitable. We were sick about it. When we asked about rewriting a few of the words, the answer we got was an unequivocal no. It wasn't long before we heard this same song on the radio recorded by another group, moving toward number one on the charts. The record company frowned on us all the more for deciding against their recommendations. Two weeks later, "One Bad Apple," our first big hit, fell into our laps.

Sticking up for my unpopular religious beliefs in a world full of entertainers has never been as difficult for me as sticking up for deeper, inner principles among my own family. Though we've sung and danced side by side on the stage over the years, we've had struggles and heartaches to overcome, like any family. As I've shown, financial ups and downs, health problems, and family disagreements coincided with our performing life. Having been brought up under the credos *All for one and one for all* and *The show must go on,* it's been a long process learning to distinguish God's will for me from my feelings of loyalty to my family.

I'm gradually learning that we never have to sacrifice even an ounce of our deeply-held beliefs for anything or anyone. Though we can do what seems best to help others, it's never beneficial to become a doormat. When we do, we not only compromise our own integrity, but we may also hinder someone else's growth. Here's an example.

Five-year-old Donny joined us on *The Andy Williams Show* after we four boys had been there for about a year. He immediately stole the show. Maybe this is when our old saying, "It doesn't matter who's out front, as long as it's an Osmond," came about. We stepped back, and generally speaking, we were proud of our gifted baby brother and grateful to be a part of something successful. From then on, just about every move we made, every step we took, every word we said on stage was calculated to spotlight Donny. It worked. It was show biz, but it wasn't a healthy way of life off stage.

Back in 1991, I was recording a solo album for Curb Records when a song called "I'll be Good to You" came to my attention. When Mike Curb brought it to me for review, I fell in love with the song. It was sure to be a hit. The only problem was that Donny had recently recorded it himself. There were no legal issues involved, but I felt uneasy.

I went ahead and recorded the song. My contract with Mike Curb was in the final stages of getting inked, the masters mixed and ready to go. Excitement over "I'll Be Good to

You" had reached a high pitch. I was informed by my attorney that my entire deal was riding on this one song. But every time I thought about Donny, a knot formed in my stomach. I felt I needed to have a visit with him about the song, even if it turned out to be a sensitive issue. I didn't imagine much of a problem; still, I needed to confront it head-on.

Talking with Donny, I was sorry to find out that he did not want me to use the song under any circumstances. He was hoping to release it as a single and didn't want it on my album. We went over different possibilities, but couldn't come to a resolution. In my disappointment and confusion, I handled things poorly. I hung up the phone feeling our good relationship would be damaged if I went forward with my contract.

I took my wife Mary by the hand, got in the car, and drove out into the desert. We rode for hours, discussing the problem, trying to gain perspective. Words and tears fell heavy. To me, the situation seemed hopeless. Even my prayers were clouded by the fact that I might displease my brother. Filled with doubts and fears, I turned the car toward home declaring to Mary that I just couldn't handle the conflict anymore.

The following day, I cancelled my contract with Curb Records. I felt like I'd been shot in the head. Everything I'd worked for, my original songs and months of effort, had been tossed in the garbage — all over my reluctance to make waves.

Looking back, I realize now that if I had gone forward with my plans, there may have been some strained feelings between Donny and me, but ultimately the results of calmly standing up for myself would have been beneficial. God expects us to be our own best friend, to set clear, reasonable boundaries that we don't allow others to cross. We can do this thoughtfully and tactfully, all the while keeping our cool and treating others with respect.

The belief involved here is that we matter, each of us. We're entitled to our feelings and opinions, our hopes and our dreams. If others find this belief system inconvenient, it is really their problem—a problem they can grow from if they choose.

We're actually here to provide these kinds of opportunities for each other, consciously or unconsciously. When we become aware of giving someone else a chance to grow through taking care of ourselves, we can pray for them. But our primary job is to courageously choose to remain in tune with the spirit of truth that confirms we are of immeasurable value. Each of us is a deserving recipient of all the good feelings and fulfillment that striving to know God's will can give.

Once again, if we are grumbling or unsettled, we are the one with the problem that needs addressing immediately. I see now that the drama surrounding the album situation could have been avoided. My feelings of doubt and fear were not from a loving Heavenly Father. He wants us to be confident in our great worth and the worth of all his children. Incidentally, Donny never did release the song as a single like he had planned.

I'm glad to know that though I can learn from past weaknesses, there is no use condemning myself. God is only concerned with our progress. Once we desire to do God's will, our foibles will come tumbling out of the shadows into the light. We can rejoice that we have been made aware of them, thank our Father that we have a Savior, and press forward filled with love.

In the '70s, the Osmond name was often exposed to ridicule in show business circles. But not everyone in the industry shunned us. There were those who were gracious, welcoming, and encouraging. They may not have agreed with us on everything, but they respected and appreciated our efforts and interest in music.

Journal, age 18

I just met Elvis Presley. He reminds me of an older brother. We are using his clothes designer. He loves talking to Mother and has been reading The Book of Mormon.

Journal, age 23

We met Paul McCartney in France. Paul has been a real friend lately. He even defended us to others who have been taking potshots at our music. When the door opened to Paul's hotel room, it was magic. Mary was especially mesmerized by him. But what was even funnier was seeing Paul's daughter go crazy staring into my brother Donny's eyes!

Journal, age 24

While performing at Earls Court in London we got word that Led Zeppelin wanted to say hi. We were elated! We happened to be using their sound system since they were playing in the same arena that night. We showed up and were escorted back stage to meet them. What nice people. We had a chance to meet their families and walk on stage with them.

What do you believe about yourself? What are your belief systems and values? I hope you cultivate the truth that you are a valued child of God, an heir to all his blessings. Sometimes old habits are hard to break. There's been too much media exposure. The artificial lights shine too bright and we can't see clearly. With perseverance and prayer, we'll gradually come closer to seeing who we truly are and discovering what God wants for us.

Out of Step

WEAKNESS

One of the biggest production numbers we ever did back on *The Andy Williams Show* was the song and dance routine "High Is Better Than Low." We rehearsed it all week trying to get it perfect for live TV. The choreography had us climbing big boxes stacked on top of each other on a certain cue. On the day of the show, there went the countdown, the cameras rolled, and we started dancing

Things went fine until I got to the very top. The box I was standing on suddenly collapsed. I fell right through it. Grabbing at the box's edge with my fingertips, I glanced below, horrified to find myself dangling over a black hole. While my brothers kept dancing, never missing a step, there was nothing for me to do but hold on. Seven minutes later the number ended and everybody ran up to see if I was still hanging in there. I was.

I like to think of this little story as a foreshadowing of a challenge I would experience later in life. It wasn't until I was in my 30s that I was diagnosed with a chemical deficiency causing manic depression.

In my early childhood, life was predictable and structured. Yes, I had my farm chores, music lessons, rehearsing, and performing, but there was also time to relax with the family and even go fishing now and then. I was eight when we signed on with Andy Williams and the pressure began to mount. I first remember being unable to sleep in my early teen years. I'd lie awake for hours trying to sort out what was happening, trying to keep pace with my life.

Often my brothers and I went sleepless for nights on end talking and planning, working on themes, and writing songs. When a project was finished we'd totally crash. But the letdown I experienced was more than physical exhaustion. It felt like despair. The feelings of gloom and doom were unexplainable; after all, the work was done and being met with approval.

Throughout adulthood, my highs and lows occurred frequently. I underwent an unpredictable series of extreme mood swings lasting a day, several days, and sometimes even weeks at a time. My lows left me immobilized and unproductive. I pulled into a shell of self-doubt, guilt, and resentment. Negative thoughts played over and over in my mind as real as any cassette tape: "You're no good, you'll never make it, you can't do it, you're worthless." During these times, nothing anyone said could correct my distorted perception. Suicidal notions, typical of manic depression, also played a part occasionally.

My highs were just the opposite. I seemed to soar with energy and creativity. Unlimited ideas, plans, and dreams popped out of nowhere. Sleep became unnecessary. I could work effortlessly all day and through the night. I felt invincible; there was nothing I couldn't accomplish.

I remember one such period when Mary and I were on a vacation in Hawaii. One night I couldn't sleep. While lying there in the darkness, for some reason my mind became totally focused on the emotion and drama of the early pioneers of my Church. In the mid-1800s, they traveled by covered wagon and hardcart to a place where they could worship God without persecution. I pictured them as they ferried rivers, crossed plains, and climbed mountain passes to settle in the Salt Lake Valley wilderness.

Every cell of my brain tuned in on developing an artistic portrayal of this event. In my mind's eye, I constructed the sets, imagined the dialogue, and saw hundreds of children singing and dancing and playing instruments in a huge outdoor setting. Over the course of three sleepless days and nights, I completed writing the Pioneer Youth Pageant. Just as I envisioned, it was later performed on football fields, several times, both in Utah and in Branson, Missouri.

But high or low, the side effects of these extremes were inevitable. My low moods left me disillusioned and exhausted. Sometimes I found myself unable to finish a project. During highs, I sometimes made snap decisions that later turned out poorly. Worst of all, relationships suffered because of my unpredictable behavior. Just ask Mary. She knows the challenge of living alongside a person suffering from manic depression.

People ask me how I continued to perform on stage as I struggled through these exaggerated hills and valleys. It was difficult. But I had been taught since I could sing a simple song that the show must go on. That entertainment business ethic left me no way out. I put a smile on my face and hit the stage, high or low.

Up until the time I was diagnosed, I didn't fully understand why I had been experiencing such a roller coaster of emotions. Though I cried out to my Heavenly Father continually and sometimes even checked myself into the hospital during a severe depressive mode, I didn't have a clue why I couldn't seem to stay on an even keel. I figured it was just an inability to pace myself, to stay in step like everybody else, and that I could control it if I just worked hard enough at it. Even so, I was often miserable and made those around me miserable too.

Not surprisingly, it was my long-suffering wife Mary who finally insisted I seek professional help. It wasn't easy admitting I needed serious medical intervention. I didn't like the idea of having to take medication just to keep my own moods from destroying me while everyone else around me seemed to sail along unconcerned with any such inner turmoil. I was my own worst enemy. Fighting my pride, I turned to the Spirit of the Lord for guidance. Finally I learned, through many prayers and a wrenching change of heart, that medical help was necessary for me to be a better instrument in God's hands. Even after painfully submitting to my Heavenly Father's will, my patience and faith were tried through many months of experimentation with different medications, dosages, and side effects before the doctors were satisfied with my treatment.

In the years since my moods have stabilized, I find myself wondering how differently things may have turned out if I had been diagnosed and treated earlier in my life. Would the songs have been written, *The Donny and Marie Show* produced, the Osmond Studio lost? After all, I was a part of every success and a part of every failure. Surprisingly, those things don't seem to matter. In God's perfect charity, He saw me languishing in my lows and soaring in my highs and loved me all the same. What matters is where I am today. I know there are some conditions over which we have no control. God will guide us as we accept these conditions and, through faith, attempt to cope with them.

I'm reminded of one of our family vacations that turned out completely differently than we had planned. Not many years ago for Father's Day, Mary and the kids planned a trip to a favorite camping spot in the Utah mountains. An excited family raring for fun picked me up straight from the airport as I was returning from a two-month stint in Branson and Nashville. My oldest son Travis and his wife Maggon were already on the mountain setting up camp when we arrived.

But just as we were settling in, dark clouds rolled in, the wind picked up, and heavy rain began to hammer the campground. We discussed our options. Should we pack up and get off the mountain right away, or weather the unexpected storm however severe it became? We decided to head home before the storm got any worse. We rehooked the trailer to the back of the diesel truck, loaded up the car, and piled into the Suburban.

The storm worsened. Our dirt road quickly turned to slick mud. I was driving the car, or trying to. We slid back and forth until we found ourselves stuck knee-deep. Abandoning the car, we headed toward the Suburban Mary was driving. She was having her troubles, too, staying on the muddy road, even with four-wheel drive.

Just then, Travis showed up in the truck, but without the trailer. Unknown to the rest of us, the trailer had jackknifed and lost traction. To his horror, Travis found the trailer slipping down a cliff, threatening to pull the truck with it. He was able to release the trailer from the hitch just in time before it careened down the slope and wrecked below.

More determined than ever to get my family off the mountain and out of danger, I took the lead in the Suburban. By this time what was once a tree-lined mountain road had become a flood of moving water, mud, and debris. When I hit the ditches on either side, I gunned the engine, praying for some traction. We hit tree trunks head-on and ripped off low pine branches. This continued for two miles until we made it to the main highway. But where was Travis? His headlights in my rear view mirror had vanished.

Peering through the rain, I saw Heather running toward us. She had been in the truck with Travis and Maggon who had told her to go ahead and tell us they couldn't keep the truck on the road and were worried something would happen. At that point, the truck came into our view. We watched as it tipped into a huge rut as if in slow motion. As Travis pushed on the gas pedal, fence wire wrapped around the drive shaft. It wasn't going anywhere. Travis and Maggon abandoned the truck and made their way toward us on foot. We all squeezed into the Suburban and headed for home. The trailer was destroyed, the truck and car stuck in the mud, our vacation ruined. But having survived a horrendous storm, we were filled with nothing but gratitude to our Heavenly Father.

I see that this earth life is designed to give us experience at every turn, the unexpected along with the expected. Dancing confidently on those TV set boxes, I didn't know the floor would suddenly collapse under my feet. In the case of our Father's Day camp out, just as in my bouts with manic depression, I couldn't always predict a storm, know how long it would last, or how severe it would be.

These kinds of things happen to everybody to some degree. At those times, our job is to grab hold with our fingertips and hang on, even as we dangle over a dark hole. During moments of greatest struggle or pain, maybe all God wants us to do is take one breath of air into our lungs, and then another. If we are looking to Him in our extremity, we are exercising a fundamental faith in a loving Heavenly

Father that the frightening, uncertain time will pass. Armed with this faith, no matter how small or simple, we access a power far beyond our own.

Somewhere along the road of my untreated manic depressive condition, with all its ups, downs, twists, and turns, I could have sunk to a dysfunctional state or become a suicide statistic. I might have left behind muddy un-answered questions and emotional scars on my loves ones' hearts. But I stand as a testimony of God's love. There is hope. If you are struggling with emotions you don't under-stand, it may be necessary to surrender pride, exercise your agency, and act on the belief that you are of infinite worth in order to get help.

I don't always know for sure what the Lord expects of me each day, but I always seek to know His will. I agreed to come to earth and take on all these customized challenges. The question is, am I willing to let my weaknesses, my flaws, and my afflictions bring me closer to God? Even my missteps are part of His divine choreography aimed at my growth and progression.

Singing Lead

RESPONSIBILITY

Just when we think we've learned all the steps, just when we're patting ourselves on the back for making it through the show, just when we're enjoying the applause, another unknown challenge even more difficult may be just around the corner. Why is it, sometimes, that one disaster follows another? Because, as they say in show business, it ain't over until the fat lady sings.

Journal, age 19

We got off the plane in Detroit today and while we were waiting, I was walking through the airport thinking I was all alone. Wrong! All of a sudden screams roared out. I turned around to see a bunch of girls attacking me. They had me on the ground in seconds ripping at me. When the Security finally got there, I found I had no shirt on. It was completely gone.

This wasn't the only time I lost my shirt, figuratively speaking. It was about fifteen years after we lost the

Osmond Studios that I experienced another devastating financial crisis, this time on my own. Almost simultaneously, my personal finances and my health hit bottom. I checked into Duke University Hospital, but doctors were stumped at my condition. My body had shut down and nothing they prescribed seemed to be working.

Over the years I've dealt with a variety of health problems, from eczema and diabetes to invasive surgeries and manic depression. Though some are hereditary weaknesses, it now became obvious that my perception of what was happening in my life was reflected in my physical and emotional health. Losing sleep, eating poorly, and fixating on financial problems all contributed to serious health concerns.

Putting business ventures aside, perhaps my most damaging mistakes occurred in lending great amounts of money to friends without receiving adequate security for repayment. Now creditors, familiar with my famous family, refused to work with me under the impression that I could easily come up with the resources to cover my debts, not realizing my family was in no position to help. I felt abandoned by friends, family, even God. As I lay in my hospital bed, I was sure I had made too many mistakes and comitted too many sins, and I needed to be punished.

Journal, age 20

Chuck Norris hit me while we were sparring today. He said, "Are you ready for this?" I held my stomach tight and said, "Go for it." I didn't even see it coming when he smacked me in the chest. I landed on the floor, the wind totally knocked out of me. I saw stars and heard bells and wished I were dead. I have never been hit that hard, ever!

When my health stabilized, I returned home with feelings of discouragement and humiliation. Though my immediate family offered comfort and support and a willingness to tighten their belts, I allowed myself to become overwhelmed by what others were surely thinking and saying about my character and integrity. Every time I went to the grocery store in our small town or filed in to church on Sunday, I felt eyes boring through me, people judging me, groups huddled together talking about me. I began to keep my distance. It was a dark time.

Does God allow these dark times or do we bring them upon ourselves? Perhaps both. We're here to experience darkness so we can know light. How long we stay in the darkness is up to us. Sometimes we have to fall low enough or feel miserable enough to want to change. When that time comes, we are now ready to use our agency to take charge and turn to God. One long night, I started over.

Journal, age 43

I'm writing this at 5:00 A.M. Through the night I felt a major shift in my heart. Because of the financial stress I'm under and the health conditions I'm battling,

I decided to take my situation to the Lord and ask for serious help. For years I have poured out my heart in prayer with great emotion, but this time I felt the need to detach personally and search the scriptures for truths and insight and to pray for instruction instead of pleading for miraculous solutions to my problems. I am changed tonight. My thoughts are clear. I no longer see these adversities the same way. In fact, I welcome them now. I realize that everything that happens, good or bad, is part of my overall growth and experience on earth. As long as I'm trying to do the right things for the right reasons, I'm moving in the right direction. All Heavenly Father asks is that I remain steadfast in Christ.

As a member of the Osmond Brothers, I mostly sing lead. It's a big responsibility to watch the pitch, carry the melody, and maintain the tone. It strikes me that we are each our own lead singer. Daunting as it may seem, taking charge of our own lives, independent of any other human being, is an emancipating prospect. If we take a spiritual view of this personal responsibility for ourselves, it becomes even more exciting.

At times, I am prone to get distracted from my source of spiritual strength and lose my way, as we all are. Every one of us needs a rescuer to save us from our failings and to light the way home. Christ is that way. His life and teachings offer insight into how we can become like him. For example, he always turned to his Father for help in difficult times. He also turned to Him in times of peace and success, giving all the glory, or credit, to his Father. He promises us, because of his atoning sacrifice, that he is in a position to plead our case before the Father, to pay our debts, to bind up our wounds, to make us clean. I believe Christ can do this for us. Our job is to exercise just a particle of faith and press forward in that hope.

In the case of my finances, things didn't turn out the way I planned. Instead of dwelling on my errors, I had the option of turning them over to Christ. This was possible, even though others may have lost their trust in me and friends may have shunned me. All this had nothing to do with my worth as a child of God. In the midst of my troubles, I could choose to be filled with peace.

So what was my responsibility? Didn't I have to ultimately take the blame for my financial difficulties? Wasn't it all my fault?

I try to look at my shortcomings from another perspective. Though I do sing lead in my own life's concert, I am making God's music. Everything I have belongs to God. He gives me the very breath that enables me to sing. With this in mind, the question, *Who does my money really belong to?* arises. It's God's, of course, and He is merely giving me the assignment to make good use of it to glorify Him.

What happens when, through poor management, risky ventures, neglect, or even through no fault of our own, we misuse or lose God's money? How does He feel about it? I think it's safe to say He doesn't care so much about the money as He does about us and our relationship with Him. Like any kind parent, He wants us to feel His love, learn from our mistakes, and try again. Because of His infinite charity, He does not condemn us, as we so easily condemn ourselves. As we feel this love and encouragement, we are more able to disregard the untruths others may be thinking, change our own self-condemning thoughts, and begin to pick up the pieces.

As I've mentioned, dwelling on past mistakes only creates feelings and emotions that distort our thoughts. The truth is everyone makes mistakes. We've bought our ticket and now find ourselves thrown together in a crowded, noisy, rock and roll concert of human imperfections. Our creator's plan is that we'll use our own weaknesses and the weaknesses of others to learn something of His love.

At times in my life I've felt like a lead singer on what seems to be a very lonely stage. But when I look behind me, I find I have God's whole orchestra and chorus backing me up, His Son amplifying my song to make it complete.

High Energy

HEART

Journal, age 18

Toronto, Canada. I can't even begin to explain what just happened. We had a charter bus taking us to our concert tonight. When we got outside the auditorium, thousands of fans were waiting for us. They surrounded the bus. We couldn't budge. The driver became extremely nervous. He started yelling at the fans to move away and panic started to set in. The bus driver hit the gas pedal. I think we ran over people. That's right, we felt the bumps as we ran over them.

Journal, age 21

Akron, Ohio. We played the stadium tonight and thousands of fans came out to see us. Security wasn't good and didn't have a sturdy fence to protect the front of the stage. When the show started, the fans charged the stage and broke the fence to pieces. It was very sad. Many were literally stabbed. There was a place back

*stage where the wounded were placed. We had to stop
the show about five times to keep the crowd from hurting themselves.*

Crazed fans, caught up in mob mentality, compromised their own safety as well as ours. It seemed that their
object was to make any kind of connection with us: to tear
our clothes, grab our hair, scratch us, or even hit us with
used flash cubes. At one concert, a big hunk of metal came
flying out of nowhere and hit the stage dangerously close to
Alan. Ironically, it had the word *love* inscribed on it.

As much as I appreciate our loyal fans, to this day I
wonder about people who risk their personal safety and
devote such high energy to idolizing other human beings. It
could be we're all prone to place our hearts in things of
exaggerated value or little importance.

There was a time in my life when I got caught up in
wearing jewelry, driving fancy cars, and doing big business
deals nonstop, day after day, night after night. Later I realized my materialistic, workaholic lifestyle wasn't worth the
time I was missing with my wife and kids. As I neglected
my relationship with God by getting caught up in worldly
distractions, my relationships with the people I loved most
suffered.

We can make a long list of negative distractions.
Addictions and destructive behaviors of all kinds plague
our society today. These include inordinate debt and mate-
rialism, obsession with entertainment, sexual fantasies,

pornography, infidelity, homosexuality, body worship, obesity and eating disorders, depression, illegal and prescription drug addiction, and domestic violence.

In many cases, involvement in these indulgences is a result of physical disorders or past abuses done to us. Professional help may be needed to correct a history of wrong ideas and damaging thought patterns behind these behaviors. Aside from clinical cases, I believe today's media-influenced, greed and power-driven world is enough to make us merely forget who we are. Easily distracted as we humans can be, we allow ourselves to get caught up in counterfeit values and worthless trends. Perhaps we hope to find meaning in life, or relief from pain and pressure in temporary excitement, attention, or stimulation.

Our own thinking is the key to changing where we put our energy and overcoming useless or destructive behaviors. We can change our distorted thoughts by continually replacing them with truth. If we're going to tell ourselves something, why not make it something true? For example, if I'm feeling down, I try to focus my thoughts on God's love for me, apart from my circumstances or failings.

I believe that the most effective way to change thoughts is by prayer, simply because in the exercising of even a small amount of faith we call upon powers greater than our own. And God assures us the heavens are open twenty-four hours a day. We can pray about who we are and about God's love for us as often as we desire, anywhere, anytime. Miracles will result, if only in the private corners of our hearts, that will change where we put our efforts and spend our time.

If you are reading a book like this one, you are probably putting most of your time and energy into worthwhile activities such as developing and sharing talents and skills, contributing to society, volunteering, raising a family, improving relationships, and serving in church and community organizations. Putting our hearts into these types of things is often personally fulfilling and rewarding, but there's another subtle change that can occur inside us that can cause our good efforts to benefit our lives even more.

I've mentioned how all-encompassing my performing life has been—the endless rehearsing and perfection required of us when we were young. Dancing as hard as we sang, we practiced our choreography until it was so tight we practically moved as one person. A great deal of emphasis was placed on high energy levels, stamina, and pacing. We learned to gauge every motion toward maximum positive audience reaction. Along with singing and dancing, sometimes we threw in some extra antics audiences loved, like breaking boards using karate moves. Sometimes we got a little too enthusiastic.

Journal, age 23

We are at Indianapolis, Indiana where 16,000 people attended our concert. In the middle of our karate number, Alan got too close and hit Jay in the nose. Blood spurted everywhere. Poor Jay was stunned. No one knew what to do, so we decided to stop the show. Alan went up to the microphone and said we'd be right back. When we left the stage everything stopped. The silence was amazing. Offstage we gave Jay a healing blessing and first aid. In ten minutes we were back, Jay with a big bandage on his nose. The crowd went crazy. After the show Jay went to the hospital and got his nose reset.

Grateful for the opportunity to make what we hoped was a positive influence in the world, we gave it all we had, and then some, and our efforts paid off in popularity and worldly success. Even so, it didn't last. The Osmonds' experience with pop music is a perfect example of how temporary and unreliable earthly rewards can be. Our popularity peaked and began to subside within a decade. Perhaps you have put all the energy you had into something only to find it fail or fade. This doesn't mean we throw up our hands in despair. There's a bigger reason beyond the lures of this life that can give meaning to our efforts.

It was 1988 and George Bush was out on the campaign trail speaking all over the country. The Republican National Committee contacted the Osmonds, asking if we would perform and say a few words at a key rally in Florida. We agreed to do it, but as the day approached, I was the only brother available.

Thousands of people showed up to the rally in Florida. The Secret Service informed me that I had forty-five minutes before I would be introducing the next President of the

United States and that I was the only person approved to hold a microphone during the entire event. They were worried that somebody would take command of the stage and make some negative comments. The microphone would go directly from me to George Bush.

On a roll for nearly an hour, I told every story I knew. Finally, I felt a tap on my shoulder that I thought signified my time was up, but a voice in my ear informed me that Mr. Bush was going to be another 50 minutes. "So, stretch!" said the voice. I couldn't give the microphone to anyone, I was out of material, and I had to keep the huge crowd energized and excited for Mr. Bush's appearance.

Sweating, my heart beating fast, I spotted a little old country band playing in the very back of the field. I asked one of the Security guys to hop in a police car and see what he could do about bringing those musicians up front. In five minutes a five-piece band sat on the stage playing songs I had never heard before. I sang them anyway, making up words and melodies. We were about twenty minutes into it when I felt another tap on the shoulder.

"Stretch it out one more hour. He's really late."

I couldn't believe it. How could I keep this crowd occupied for another hour? I started a human wave. I split the crowd in half and challenged them to wave competitions and cheering contests. We held sing-a-longs and stand-up comedy acts. After what seemed like an eternity, a convoy of police cars appeared with sirens blaring and lights flashing. They gave me the signal and, much to my relief, I announced, "Ladies and Gentlemen, the next President of the United States, George Bush."

Suddenly, he was on stage giving me a hearty hug and whispering in my ear, "I owe you one."

Why are we sweating buckets on this stage? What are we waiting and hoping for? Is it worth it, putting our hearts into our daily activities, whatever they may be, sometimes vamping as we look forward to some temporary relief, enjoyment, or reward?

Often we do not feel equally compensated by the amount of blood, sweat, and tears we put into our efforts. We don't get quite enough praise or feedback. People aren't quite excited or effusive enough. There's just not enough payback. Unless there is another source. Can we do the same mundane things and receive fulfilling spiritual benefits?

There's a sweet reward awaiting us if we put our hearts into what matters most. Though it may sound abstract, it's possible to do every good thing we happen to be doing out of gratitude and love for God. In return, we'll not only enjoy the fruits of our accomplishments, but we'll also be treated to the exquisite miracle of feeling His love, like a warm hug, on a continual basis.

What's required is a subtle tweak in our motivation, a tweak that can bring tremendous spiritual results. As you and I fill our lives with everyday tasks, service to others, and worthwhile activities, instead of doing them out of obligation, fear, or a desire to feel of value, we can do them out of love for our Creator to whom we owe our every breath.

With every accomplishment, large or small, I try to remember to immediately thank Him in a private prayer for the opportunity to serve Him with the resources He provides.

Wherever I place my highest energy, my devotion, or my heart, is where I find my real treasure lies. If my treasure lies in love of God and His love for me, I find strength and creativity beyond my own, enabling me to stretch another hour, another day, another year, when I think I have nothing left to give. With our souls filled with truth and gratitude, we'll no longer slip into the darkness of negative behaviors. We'll be blessed with elusive peace and well-being the whole world craves. "Well done," our Heavenly Father will assure us, not just at the end of the show, but all along the way.

Love Song

GRACE

Journal, age 20

For weeks my brothers and I have been working on a project called The Plan. A lot of inspiration has been pouring out and the Spirit has been strong. Alan just wrote a song called "Before the Beginning" and the more I hear it the more I like it. It's going to be interesting to see how our record company reacts to this project.

Mike Curb has agreed to let us release The Plan but we have to tone down some of the songs. This is going to be a great message.

Today all our work on The Plan went up in flames. The only room to burn up in the hotel was ours, the room that had our work. We have no back up records of any of it. We are so sick. There are no remaining tapes, no paper trail. We had a five-inch thick manual that contained every note and word, and now it's gone. We've already decided to rewrite.

We did rewrite *The Plan,* a themed album of original songs. It was recorded and released. Though it was our best work musically, it flopped commercially, probably because we let it be known that it was about our religious beliefs. Perhaps if we had kept quiet about the underlying meanings of the songs, most people would never have made the connection. That didn't seem right to us. More than anything, we wanted to share the good news of the gospel of Jesus Christ. Of all the recordings we ever did, two songs on this album are among my all-time favorites: "Before the Beginning" and "Let Me In."

Before the beginning we were living
Oh so far away from here
And we called it home but didn't stay
We knew that we could leave one day and cry

Before the beginning we were willing
To lay aside who we had been
And take a chance to slip away
Or make it back to home one day, what for?

Ever since we came to be
With the plan we've learned to see
We alone would guide our destiny

In the beginning, we'd be living
As we would be, He once was

To look at Him, to look at me
And think some day like Him I'll be, what more?

Ever since we came to be
With the plan we learned to see
We control infinity
What more?
What more?
— Alan, Wayne, and Merrill Osmond, "Before the Beginning," 1973

The Osmonds may have been in a position to spread the word of God on a grand scale. In raising my own family, I've learned I don't have to produce a CD to share Christ's good news and make a dramatic difference. Home is the best place of all to discuss and apply our convictions—the positive, far-reaching effects of which may be immeasurable.

One day our little daughter Sheila was playing with a ball in the house. Mary told her to take it outside, explaining that there were breakable things in the house that we wouldn't want damaged. On her way out, Sheila bounced the ball one more time. It hit the wall, ricocheted toward a treasured china cabinet, and shattered the glass door with a great crash. Mary came running into the room.

"Sheila!" cried Mary. "I told you not to throw that ball in the house! Now look what you've done! This is going to cost hundreds of dollars!"

From the other room I heard Sheila attempt to apologize, but Mary was beside herself. The next thing I knew, Sheila stood beside my chair, her eyes filled with tears.

159

"Will you forgive me, Daddy?" she asked. I pulled her onto my lap.

"It was wrong to bounce the ball in the house, wasn't it?" I said.

"Yes."

"When you don't mind your mother, bad things can happen. Can you pay for that glass door?"

"No."

Suddenly, this felt like a good opportunity to teach a sweet and marvelous principle. I took out my checkbook. Estimating the cost of repairing the cabinet, I filled it out and signed it, Mr. Mercy. I handed the check to Sheila.

"Since you are sorry and have no way to pay, I would like to help. This is for you to give to Mother," I said. Sheila's eyes widened. "It's the same as Jesus does for all of us. When we ask, he is always there to help." I got a big hug before she jumped off my lap and ran to her mother waving the check in the air. The story of Mr. Mercy became a favorite in our family.

A few songs on *The Plan* album did well as singles. "Let Me In" was one of them. It comes across as an emotional love song, swelling with an orchestra-full of passion. But like all the songs in this collection, it has a hidden meaning. What appears to be a typical love song, similar to many others you hear on the radio, was purposefully written with something besides romantic love in mind. It's about reaching out to the love our Savior offers, about choosing to feel the warmth of his redeeming grace.

It's a funny thing about pop love songs. If you shift your focus the slightest bit, most of them can apply to our personal relationship with our Savior rather than a romantic relationship. Here are some lyrics to "Let Me In." Try it.

Loving you can be so easy
Loving you can make me warm
Ever since the day I left you
I tried but I just can't get you out of my mind
Thought that I could do without you
Thought I had to look around
But now that I know I need you
I promise that I'll never leave you
Won't you please let me in
Let me in your arms again
Let me give my love to you once more
Let me love you
Take me in, take me in your arms to stay
And I'll never go away again
Cause I love you
       – Alan, Wayne, and Merrill Osmond, "Let Me In," 1973

Isn't it interesting? Love songs can be converted into Christ songs, just as everything on this earth testifies of him—if we'll only see things that way. All our Father in Heaven and His son ask is that we turn to them. The miracle is, in doing so every facet of our lives becomes more enjoyable, meaningful, and abundant.

In the scriptures, we read a lot about repentance. And though we often think of repentance in terms of terrible sins that need confessing to our bishop or priest or pastor, this is not necessarily the case. Repentance means to turn back to God, to change our hearts much like the way we changed the meaning of the words of an ordinary love song. It means feeling divine love and acceptance apart from the good or bad things we do, or the good and bad things that happen. In feeling this love and acting upon it, we will not only lose all desire to do evil, we will automatically be more effective in accomplishing more good. Repenting is the difference between making ourselves our God, and making Heavenly Father our God.

Many of us think it sounds too good to be true, that it's too easy, that the answers to all our complex problems can't be solved by something as simple as a humble prayer. We decide we must become our own saviors by driving ourselves into the ground, or by finding ways, however subtle, to punish ourselves and even the score.

Christ warns us not to be distracted and slothful just because of the easiness, or simplicity, of his gospel. Unlike us, he is perfectly aware of our shortcomings and our weaknesses, and also of our infinite potential. He wants us empowered, not by confidence in ourselves but by confidence in him and his atoning gift.

By repenting, yielding to his will, or simply turning to him, we begin to humble ourselves, to rely on a power greater than our own. His spirit opens our eyes and we begin to see where we need to improve. We will also start to treat ourselves and others with the same kind of patience and long-suffering he offers. Cushioned by this mercy, I find I react differently to my humanness and the humanness of others, knowing our failings are only meant to remind us to turn to our Savior, to see the light, and to bask in his love.

You know how a hit song you especially like to listen to over and over on your radio or CD player becomes automatically ingrained in your mind? In the privacy of your car or home, you can belt out the song along with the artist as if it were your own recording. It's the same with gospel principles. By spending time praying about and pondering these pure truths, they can become fixed in our minds and hearts like the words of that favorite pop song you can't get out of your head even if you want to.

These Christlike thoughts will come to our aid when we need them. We'll know how to handle a feeling or problem the way Heavenly Father would want us to. We'll remember who we are and why we're here. More and more, we'll turn to our most reliable source.

If we're humbly striving for a pure heart, full of love for God and all men, we can be sure God will provide us with miracles. These miracles may be dramatic but, more often than not, they will be along the lines of strength to endure, peace of mind, and creative ideas to help us cope with or resolve a dilemma. When I truly recognize these quiet miracles in my daily life, they are as dramatic to me as Christ causing the blind to see with a touch of his hand. I believe the greatest miracle of all is the change the Spirit of the Lord can cause in a person's heart.

I am learning to give the Spirit credit for every kind of miracle in my life, even if it's just a quiet feeling of courage and well-being amid a difficult challenge. As I strive to recognize every good feeling as a gift from a loving God, to whom all things belong, I desire to thank Him immediately. By giving God acknowledgment for everything—my accomplishments, my joys, and my trials—I've come to find meaning in every experience.

Isn't God's love incredible? If we hang in there, we find out that dead ends and failures become our greatest blessings. Whatever our circumstances, God invites us to see them as part of His plan. We can live quiet, meaningful inner lives founded on the assurance that everything we encounter is essential to our overall growth and experience on earth, looking forward to a grander life to come. Filled with faith in my Heavenly Father's plan and reliance on Christ, I welcome it all.

I've sung a lot of songs in my life on a lot of stages. As a small boy in a bow tie and suspenders, I blended my voice with my brothers' in sentimental barbershop tunes. As a youth in a white, sequined jumpsuit, I belted flashy rock and roll to the rhythm of electric guitars and crashing drums. As a young man, I harmonized to Christmas carols with five brothers and my sister Marie. As an adult, I donned cowboy hat and boots and drawled country ballads to the twang of my banjo. Close to my heart is a collection of favorite sacred hymns recorded in recent years to the accompaniment of a single acoustic guitar.

At the present time, I regularly perform with my brothers Wayne and Jay all over the country in shows which are made up of a variety of all the types of songs I've ever sung. Everyone in our audience seems to find something to enjoy in the eclectic mix. Me, I like to think of myself as an old rocker.

In a larger sense, this mortal existence comes down to one tune, one beat, one melody. More than any other, I choose to sing the song of a divine, redeeming love with all the energy and ability given me.

𝓕inale

Journal, age 19

We made a big boo-boo today. We are working with Nancy Sinatra at the Hilton Hotel. Tonight was our first show and we were doing the big opening number with her. Well, at one point she tripped over Alan's leg and fell down on the stage. She started to cry. We tried to help her up but she pulled away. We didn't know what to do. Somebody pulled the curtain closed. In the audience sat her father Frank Sinatra, Elvis Presley, Tom Jones, and half the entertainment industry. All through the rest of the show we thought we were done for.

After the show was over there was a knock on the dressing room door and there stood two guys in suits and hats. "Mr. Sinatra wants to see you," they said. We were dying. We had no idea what was going down. Just then he walked in. All he did was thank us for being good entertainers. Boy, that made me sweat. It was my first time meeting this legend.

My Church has its "legends," too. As a young man, I often met with our Church President at the time, Spencer W. Kimball, with whom I had a close relationship. One particular time, I had an appointment with him in Salt Lake City. As I entered his outer office, it seemed curious to find four men there who invited me to sit down and began asking me all kinds of questions. This went on for quite a while until I saw President Kimball's secretary, Arthur Haycock, press a button under his desk. Suddenly, there he was, my beloved President Kimball, seeming to glow with faith and good will. Relieved, I embraced him and felt his kiss on my cheek.

We had a good visit, but it wasn't until I was driving home that I realized the significance of what had occurred. It struck me that, after we've been through our earthly experience, after we've answered all the questions and passed the test, we needn't be afraid. Just as President Kimball greeted me, our Father in Heaven will greet us, with something that will feel as personal as a holy kiss.

Now, my friends, time is up. Someone has put a shiny star on your dressing room door. The sound man says all systems are go. We've held our last minute tech meeting and you're ready to hit the stage. There goes the countdown. Suddenly, you've arrived. It's show time at Madison Square Garden and the crowd is screaming your name. You're singled out in the spotlight, just like you always dreamed. You're a star!

You, me, we're all making our debut on this bright stage called earth life. Sometimes we'll forget the words.

Sometimes we'll remember them without a glitch. Sometimes we'll trip and fall on our faces. Sometimes we'll dance effortlessly on our toes. Sometimes the crowd will scream and applaud. Sometimes the crowd will throw tomatoes.

Whatever our circumstances, the show must go on. We'll keep singing and dancing the best we know how until the curtain falls. On that day we will meet the greatest legends of all, God our Heavenly Father and His Son Jesus Christ. If we have made their love our paramount reason for performing, our welcome home will be a bigger, star-studded spectacular than we can imagine.

Order Form

Let the Reason Be Love, by Merrill Osmond

Fax orders: 801-785-9676. Send this form.

Email orders: orders@tidalwavebooks.com. Include name, address, credit card info (VISA/MC, number, name on card, expiration date)

Postal orders: Tidal Wave Books
                4476 N Wedgewood Drive
                Pleasant Grove, UT 84062, USA

Number of copies ordered: _____ x $19.95 = _____

Sales tax: Please add $1.25 sales tax for books shipped to Utah addresses: _____

Shipping and handling: $4.00 for the first book, $2.00 for additional books: _____

Total of Order:_____

Payment: Check_____   Credit card: _____Visa   _____MasterCard
Card Number: _____
Name on card: _____ Exp. date: _____

Please send to:

Name: _____
Address: _____
City: _____ State. _____ Zip: _____
Telephone: _____
Email address: _____

Please allow 4–6 weeks for delivery.